The Evils of Necessity:

Robert Goodloe ~~H~~
Moral Dilem~~ma~~

FRONTISPIECE. Harper in miniature. Watercolor on ivory by Robert Field, 1800-1801. Courtesy of the Maryland Historical Society.

TRANSACTIONS
OF THE
AMERICAN PHILOSOPHICAL SOCIETY
Held at Philadelphia
For Promoting Useful Knowledge
Vol. 87, Pt. 1

The Evils of Necessity:

Robert Goodloe Harper and the Moral Dilemma of Slavery

Eric Robert Papenfuse

American Philosophical Society
Independence Square • Philadelphia
1997

ISBN: 0-87169-871-4   Library of Congress No.: 96-84055
US ISSN: 0065-9746

For Cathy

Table of Contents

List of Maps and Illustrations

ACKNOWLEDGMENTS

OVER THE LAST FOUR YEARS numerous people have given generously of their time to assist me in completing this book. Let me begin by thanking the many archivists, curators, and librarians who patiently answered all my research queries. I was treated with extraordinary kindness at each of the institutions I visited. Deserving special recognition for their patience, hospitality, and good advice, are the staffs at the American Antiquarian Society, New-York Historical Society, New York Public Library, Pierpont Morgan Library, Princeton University Libraries, Johns Hopkins University Libraries, Maryland State Archives, and Library of Congress. Let me also extend my heartfelt gratitude to those individuals who went out of their way to offer useful suggestions and to provide me with manuscript and printed materials, especially Jennifer Bryan and Jeff Goldman of the Maryland Historical Society, Ronald Hoffman and Sally Mason of the Carroll Papers Project, William Johnston of the Walters Art Gallery, William Elder of the Baltimore Museum of Art, Shirley Bodziak of the Maryland State Archives, Laura Ceostella of the South Caroliniana Library, Conyers Bull of the Charleston Library Society, Linda McCurdy of the Duke University Library, Susan Swasta of the William L. Clements Library, Laura Monti of the Boston Public Library, Peter Drummey and Virginia Smith of the Massachusetts Historical Society, Judith Ann Schiff of Manuscripts and Archives at Yale University, and Harper's descendent, Carolyn T. Fisher, who graciously invited me into her home and shared her family's papers.

This massive undertaking never could have been completed without the financial support of Jonathan Edwards College and the Yale Graduate School, whose timely grants, fellowships, and prizes made it possible to journey to most of the institutions already mentioned. No amount of research would have sufficed without the constant willingness of my friends, family members, and fellow students to listen to my ideas, read drafts of chapters, and offer constructive criticism. Especially supportive were:Catherine Allgor, Joshua Civin, Bob Fetter, Robert Forbes, Ben Karp, David Marcus, David Papenfuse, Sallie Papenfuse, Jonathan Prosen, Andrew Siegel, and John Stauffer.

As an advisor and mentor, no one has offered me more support and encouragement than David Brion Davis. My study of Harper began as a paper for his junior seminar in the fall of 1991 and since that time it has constantly improved under his watchful care and direction. As anyone who knows Professor Davis will attest, he is a truly exceptional scholar with an unparalleled devotion to his students. For their ever-faithful interest, good humor, and enthusiasm, I wish also to thank my many other teachers who have assisted me in this project, especially Doron Ben-Atar, John Demos, Ann Fabian, David Hackett Fischer, Robert Forster, and Barbara Oberg.

In closing, four individuals deserve particular acknowledgment. My editor, Carole Le Faivre-Rochester, never doubted the importance of this work. She has spent countless hours refining my cumbersome prose and designing the final product, which you now hold in your hands. My father, Edward C. Papenfuse, has been a steady source of inspiration and guidance. As the Maryland State Archivist, it was he who first introduced me to Harper and his world, and no one has done more to show me the importance of preserving our collective heritage. Rose Thomas, with her many compelling stories of growing up in Harper, Liberia, helped remind me of the essential continuity between past and present. Finally, with unfailing love and energy Catherine Ann Lawrence has shared with me her remarkable abilities as a patient reader, careful editor, and fellow student of history. It is to her that this book is dedicated.

CHAPTER ONE

Education and the "True Religion"

ROBERT GOODLOE HARPER was born in January 1765 near Fredericksburg, Virginia. His father, Jesse, was a successful cabinet-maker, and his mother, Diana, came from a prominent local family. In 1768 the Harpers sold their 100–acre estate and moved to Granville County, North Carolina. There, on a large plantation with cattle, sheep, hogs, horses, and more than a dozen slaves, Robert and his eight sisters spent their childhood.[1] Jesse and Diana Harper were devout Presbyterians who believed that proper instruction could "Lead the Soul to God." Eager to provide their son with the finest education that the "Country could afford," they enrolled Robert in the local grammar school around the time of his tenth birthday. For five years the young student tried to fulfill his parents' expectations by immersing himself in his studies and praying to "the Almighty for...Grace." Yet during the winter of 1780–81, he renounced his parents' religious convictions, which "rendered them extremely apprehensive to the effects of a military life," in order to enlist as a volunteer in a local cavalry corps. Until "the enemy left the State, and was shut up in York Town," Harper served valiantly, critically wounding a British officer and earning the widespread respect of his peers. By the time he returned home, his "fondness for military life" had been "greatly

---

1. Diana Harper possessed a sizable dowry. In 1788 the Harper estate totaled 1,350 acres, making it one of the largest in Granville County. The family also owned 1,250 acres in Hillsborough, N. C., which were sold upon Jesse's death in 1787. See Worth S. Ray, ed., *Colonial Granville County and Its People: Loose Leaves from "The Lost Tribes of North Carolina"* (Baltimore: Southern Book Co., 1956), 300; William A. Crozier, ed., *Virginia County Records*, vol. 1, *Spotsylvania County, 1721–1800* (New York: Fox, Duffield, and Co., 1905), 202, 263; and Zae H. Gwynn, ed., *Abstracts of the Wills and Estate Records of Granville County, North Carolina, 1746–1808* (Durham, N.C.: Seeman Printery, 1973), 117, 119, 120, 134, 161, 172. Most of what historians know of Harper's early life is based upon an autobiographical essay he wrote in 1801 for Charles Carroll of Carrollton, a wealthy Maryland landowner and signer of the Declaration of Independence. Harper was courting Carroll's daughter at the time, and as a result, his story should be viewed somewhat skeptically. See RGH, Autobiography, 10 January 1801, Harper-Pennington Papers (HPP), MS. 431, Manuscripts Division, Maryland Historical Society Library (MHSL), Baltimore; Elizabeth Harper Hyde to Charles Carroll Harper, 30 April 1825, HPP, MHSL; and Bayly E. Marks, *Guide to the Microfilm Edition of the Robert Goodloe Harper Family Papers* (Baltimore: Maryland Historical Society, 1970).

inflamed."[2] After the war, as Harper would later recount, he squandered his time in "idleness and dissipation." His love of "gaming" and obsession with "fashionable gaiety" upset his distraught parents, who disparaged their son's sinful lifestyle and urged him to repent. If, as Jay Fliegelman contends, the American revolution against British tyranny took place within a broader cultural rebellion against patriarchal authority, then Harper's actions during this period of his life reflect the prevailing spirit of the times. Rejecting traditional notions of filial responsibility, he strove repeatedly to assert personal autonomy in a world that demanded constant obedience.[3] Of the opportunities available, pursuing his education offered Harper the greatest prospect of freedom while partly conforming to his parents' expectations. Although Jesse and Diana had always intended grammar school to be the limit of his training, Robert's bad habits were too much for them to endure. Hoping that Princeton's strict, Presbyterian teachers would convince him to submit to God's will, they sent Harper to the college in June 1784. "Now May the Lord Bless Y^r Pious tutors," wrote Jesse, "with Every Necessary Qualification for Carying on so Great a Work as the training of Youth Properly is, & May he Bless you also & the Rest of the Students with Grace to follow Y^r tutors Good Instructions & Examples, & Cause All things to Work together for the temporal, Spiritual, & Eternal Good of you All...."[4]

Little is known of Harper's time in New Jersey. For more than a year he refused to correspond with his family. His parents and sisters sent message after message begging him to write, but to no avail. Their letters express an anxious concern for Robert's spiritual welfare:

---

2. Jesse and Diana Harper were not alone in believing that education was "highly necessary" for the spiritual well-being of their community. In 1779 the North Carolina legislature passed an act for establishing a "seminary of learning" in Granville County. See Walter Clark, ed., *The State Records of North Carolina*, (Goldsboro, N.C.: Nash Brothers, 1907), 22: 156-58, 24: 296-97; Ruth L. Woodward and Wesley F. Craven, *Princetonians: A Biographical Dictionary, 1784–1790* (Princeton: Princeton University Press, 1991), 67; Jesse Harper to RGH, 10 March 1785, HPP, MHSL; RGH, Autobiography, HPP, MHSL; Jesse Harper to RGH, 20 October 1784, HPP, MHSL; and John S. Pancake, *This Destructive War: The British Campaign in the Carolinas, 1780–1782* (University: University of Alabama Press, 1985), 122-244.

3. RGH, Autobiography, HPP, MHSL; Letitia Harper to RGH, 19 December 1789, HPP, MHSL; Daniel Walker Howe, "The Decline of Calvinism: An Approach to Its Study," *Comparative Studies in Society and History* 14 (June 1972): 306-27; and Fliegelman, *Prodigals and Pilgrims: The American Revolution against Patriarchal Authority, 1750–1800* (Cambridge: Cambridge University Press, 1982).

4. RGH, Autobiography, HPP, MHSL; Jesse Harper to RGH, 21 November 1784, HPP, MHSL.

And now My Dear Child suffer me to put you in Mind that an Awfull Eternity is before us, & that the Judg stands at the Dore to Whome we must all Give Account (we know not how soon) of Our Words & Actions; and be forever Happy or Miserable, As we Behave here, therefore my Child be Exhorted, to Beg of the Almighty for his Grace to Assist you, & in Concurence therewith Join Your Utmost Endeavours to Shun & avoid Every Appearance of Evil, Remember the three Grand Enimies to our Salvation are always Ready to tempt us, therefore be always, Watchfull Sober, & temperate in All things, Not failing to pray to GOD for his Grace to Assist you to Conduct yourself so throug Life, as you might Otherways wish you had done when you come to die, & that you may be Enabled to doe so is the Earnest prayer of your Loving Parents.

Such rhetoric helps illuminate the somber world from which Robert was trying to escape. According to Jesse and Diana, man was a sinful creature. "GOD" was the Master "to Whome we must all Give Account," and the faithful were little more than obedient servants in his grand design.[5]

While they prayed for their son's moral salvation, Harper's parents also reassured him that they would "take care of the Boy, Horse, Saddle, & Bridle" he had left behind in Granville.[6] That the young scholar would place such value on a black servant even as he struggled to assert his own freedom vividly illustrates the striking contradictions of slavery. For Harper it must have been particularly difficult to accept the system's troubling paradoxes. Within a short time after graduating from Princeton, he wrote his sister, Letitia, that he feared their "sentiments on religion" would always differ. Her response was highly emotional:

O my Brother! the Solemn thought Sinks with weight on my Spirits, and I am ready to cry out "O Lord! are we ready to appear before thy Tremendious Bar and give that Strict account which Justice will require in that day, for which all other days were made, that day, in which the Secrets of all hearts Shall be disclosed and none will be aquited but those whose names are found writen in the Lamb's book of life,— none but those who, while on Earth, made their peace with GOD,— felt themselves wounded by the fall and Utterly Unable to do any thing in a Natural State pleasing to their Injured Maker, bewailed

---

5. Jesse and Diana Harper to RGH, 14 July 1784, HPP, MHSL; Letitia Harper to RGH, 8 October 1785, HPP, MHSL; and Frances Harper to RGH, 9 October 1785, HPP, MHSL.

6. Most likely, this allusion refers to the "negro boy" whom Harper inherited in 1787 after his father's death. See Jesse and Diana Harper to RGH, 14 July 1784, HPP, MHSL; Gwynn, 117.

their lost perishing condition, groan'd under the heavy burden of their Actual transgressions, deeply felt the Nesesity of a better rightiousness than their own, fled to a crucify'd Savior as their only refuge from the Storm of Wrath that so justly hung over their Guilty heads, cast their Sinfull helpless Souls and bodies on his Almighty Arms, receiv'd him for their Surety, rely'd on his Merits alone for justification before GOD and liv'd and died bearing the fruits of an holly Obedience to the Will and Commands of their Great Creator.["]

Letitia's letter suggests that in repudiating his family's religion, Robert had disavowed the theological rationale with which they justified slavery. According to Letitia, sin dishonored and debased humans, leaving them in a state of what the sociologist Orlando Patterson has called "social" and "spiritual death." For Harper's family, all men were sinners; all men were slaves. Only a heartfelt acceptance of God's will could free mankind from the lasting stain of Adam's fall. Indeed, since there was no correlation between temporal bondage and divine grace, slavery's existence, rather than challenging traditional Calvinist assumptions, provided a worldly paradigm for the ethereal journey from captivity to redemption.[7]

Reverend John Witherspoon, Princeton's president from 1768 until his death in 1794, viewed the peculiar institution in much the same way as Harper's family. Not only did he fail to see "any necessity" for "those who found men in a state of slavery, to make them free to their own ruin," but near the end of his life, while serving in the New Jersey legislature, he refused to support plans for immediate abolition. Ironically, it was Witherspoon's lectures on moral philosophy that instilled in Harper a pedagogical belief in personal independence antithetical to his family's understanding of the social order. As Harper read the assigned works by John Locke, Thomas Reid, and other thinkers and debated their meanings with his fellow members of the American Whig Society, he came to the conclusion that all races of mankind possessed an innate moral sense, which required cultivation. Only reason could bring such enlightenment. It was therefore essential, for one's spiritual salvation, to

7. Of course, some Calvinists became ardent abolitionists. "Yet," as David Brion Davis has argued, "it was only among New England Calvinists that traditional eschatology gave form to an anti-slavery rhetoric which challenged the Neo-Harringtonian conception of liberty, which pointed to a more radical definition of freedom, and which anticipated the 'immediatism' of the later Garrisonians." See Davis, *The Problem of Slavery in the Age of Revolution, 1770-1823* (Ithaca: Cornell University Press, 1975), 287; idem, *The Problem of Slavery in Western Culture* (Ithaca: Cornell University Press, 1966); Patterson, *Slavery and Social Death: A Comparative Study* (Cambridge: Harvard University Press, 1982); idem, *Freedom*, vol. 1, *Freedom in the Making of Western Culture* (New York: Basic Books, 1991), 327-34; and Letitia Harper to RGH, 19 December 1789, HPP, MHSL.

reject a passionate world of unthinking obedience and to pursue an educated life of rational self–interest.[8]

After graduating from Princeton in 1785 at the age of twenty, Harper moved to Charleston to study law. He was admitted to the bar the following year and soon settled in the small town of Cambridge, a growing commercial center in the South Carolina backcountry. Cambridge was in decline by 1806. Regional depression and the relocation of the county's judicial administration had inhibited the town's development. Nevertheless, hints of its past prosperity could still be found in one traveler's account:

> The town of Cambridge is nothing more than a snug little village of 15 or 20 houses and stores on the top of a small hill called Cambridge Hill. There is an area in the center of it, where stands an old brick Court House. At a little distance down the hill is the jail,—both in a neglected state. Just out of the village in a pleasant plain, quite retired from noise, is a two story brick building, which was erected for the President's House of the college; but which is now designed by the Trustees for the Academy building itself.

In Cambridge, work came slowly at first. To supplement his income, Harper may have found employment at a local school run by the Rev-

---

8. On Harper's membership in the American Whig Society, see James Morris to RGH, 5 June 1785, HPP, MHSL; *Catalogue of the American Whig Society, Instituted in the College of New Jersey, 1769* (Princeton: American Whig Society, 1845), 9; and Jacob N. Beam, *The American Whig Society of Princeton University* (Princeton: American Whig Society, 1933). On Witherspoon's influence and Princeton's curriculum during the period of Harper's studies, consult Jack Scott, ed., *An Annotated Edition of Lectures on Moral Philosophy by John Witherspoon* (Newark: University of Delaware Press, 1982), 45, 125-26, 137; Thomas Miller, ed., *The Selected Writings of John Witherspoon* (Carbondale: Southern Illinois University Press, 1990); Francis L. Broderick, "Pulpit, Physics, and Politics: The Curriculum of the College of New Jersey, 1746–1794," *William and Mary Quarterly* 6 (January 1949): 42-68; Ronald Hamowy, "Jefferson and the Scottish Enlightenment: A Critique of Garry Wills's *Inventing America: Jefferson's Declaration of Independence*," *William and Mary Quarterly* 36 (October 1979): 503-23; Roger J. Fechner, "The Godly and Virtuous Republic of John Witherspoon," in Hamilton Cravens, ed., *Ideas in America's Cultures: From Republic to Mass Society* (Ames: Iowa State University Press, 1982), 7-25; Howe, "European Sources of Political Ideas in Jeffersonian America," *Reviews in American History* 10 (December 1982): 28-44; idem, "The Language of Faculty Psychology in *The Federalist Papers*," in Terence Ball and J. G. A. Pocock, eds., *Conceptual Change and the Constitution* (Lawrence: University Press of Kansas, 1988), 107-36; Mark A. Noll, *Princeton and the Republic, 1769–1822: The Search for a Christian Enlightenment in the Era of Samuel Stanhope Smith* (Princeton: Princeton University Press, 1989), 77-98; and the essays collected in Richard B. Sher and Jeffrey R. Smitten, eds., *Scotland and America in the Age of Enlightenment* (Edinburgh: Edinburgh University Press, 1990).

6

FIGURE ONE. Harper's world from Maryland to the Carolinas. Reprinted from William Gordon, *History of the Rise, Progress, and Establishment of the Independence of the United States of America*, 1789. Photograph courtesy of the American Philosophical Society.

erend John Springer, a fellow Princeton alumnus. Little is known about this institution. Like the rest of Cambridge, it enjoyed only a brief moment of glory. By the turn of the century, many of its buildings had vanished. "They were never any thing more than mere log–studies," observed one visitor, "temporarily thrown up, till better ones could be erected—and they are now in ruins."[9]

Whatever Harper's role at the college may have been, he and Springer became good friends. It is likely that together they founded the Cambridge Friendly Society for the Encouragement of Literature in March 1787. On the group's first anniversary Harper presented a long speech in which he assailed all those who believed, as he once had, "that virtue and morality" were "idle notions." It was lunacy, he argued, to think that man was "incapable of resisting his passions, and came into the world for the purpose of gratifying them in their fullest extent." People who denied this truth found "something in religion morality and providence" which they could not "comprehend." Thus, they wrongly concluded that there was "no such thing: just as if a mole should take on himself to prove that there is no sun, because he cannot see it, or discern the difference between it and a candle."[10]

---

9. Robert Mills, writing in 1826, called the school a "respectable academy." See Mills, *Statistics of South Carolina* (Charleston, 1826), quoted in Mary Katherine Davis, "The Feather Bed Aristocracy: Abbeville District in the 1790's," *South Carolina Historical Magazine* 80 (April 1979), 139; Donald Robert Come, "The Influence of Princeton on Higher Education in the South Before 1825," *William and Mary Quarterly* 2 (January 1945), 392; James F. Jameson, ed., "The Diary of Edward Hooker, 1805-1808," *Annual Report of the American Historical Association for the Year 1896* (Washington: Government Printing Office, 1897), 884; and Joseph W. Cox, *Champion of Southern Federalism: Robert Goodloe Harper of South Carolina* (Port Washington, N. Y.: Kennikat Press, 1972), 20.

10. At Princeton's commencement Harper presented a similar oration entitled "The Proper Objects of Education." This speech won a gold medal for best essay on a given subject, but unfortunately, it has not survived. See RGH, Autobiography, HPP, MHSL; *The New Jersey Gazette*, 10 October 1785; and RGH, "A discourse on Learning," 15 March 1788, Ms. Carolyn T. Fisher Collection of Robert Goodloe Harper Papers (CTFC), SC 2360, Maryland State Archives (MSA), Annapolis, reprinted below as Appendix A. At the time of Harper's Cambridge oration, prominent statesmen such as David Ramsay and Charles Pinckney had helped foster an atmosphere conducive to educational societies within South Carolina. Both had popularized the idea of state-wide education. Pinckney had even gone so far as to advocate provisions for "the promotion of literature and the arts and sciences" and the creation of a national university at the Philadelphia Convention. See generally John Wolfe, *Jeffersonian Democracy in South Carolina* (Chapel Hill: University of North Carolina Press, 1940), 48; William A. Schaper, *Sectionalism and Representation in South Carolina* (Washington: Government Printing Office, 1901), 402; Max Farrand, ed., *The Records of the Federal Convention of 1787*, revised with a new fourth volume by James H. Hutson (New Haven: Yale University Press, 1987), 2: 322; Wilson

(continued...)

Apparently, by the time of Harper's Cambridge oration, the nature of his rebellion against parental standards had transmuted. Where he had earlier embraced sin and dissipation, he now substituted education, the medium that had allowed him to escape his parents' universe, for grace. Only learning, it seemed, could redeem humanity. In fostering the virtue and good sense needed to discharge properly "the duties of this life," "rational and true religion" prepared mankind "for the life to come." By warming and enabling the heart, it inspired the "rising generation" to act benevolently. Those who lacked knowledge were, in Harper's estimation, slaves to their ignorance. "[I]ncapable of any but coarse and sensual enjoyments" and prone "to scenes of noise and riot and senseless mirth," they were condemned to a life of sin.[11]

In the same manner that Harper rejected traditional Calvinist assumptions of human depravity, he zealously denounced popular perceptions of racial inferiority. Blacks, he proclaimed, were inherently equal to whites:

---

10. (...continued)
Smith, ed., *Theories of Education in Early America, 1655-1819* (New York: Bobbs-Merrill, 1973), 221-29; and Peter S. Onuf, "State Politics and Republican Virtue: Religion, Education, and Morality in Early American Federalism," in Paul Finkelman and Stephen E. Gottlieb, eds., *Toward a Usable Past: Liberty Under State Constitutions* (Athens: University of Georgia Press, 1991), 91-116. Ramsay, forced to temper his antislavery convictions in the inhospitable climate of the South Carolina lowcounty, was so impressed with Harper's philosophical principles and idealistic vigor that he described the Cambridge lawyer as "a well informed & well bred young gentleman who has well founded prospects of rising to distinguished importance in our rising empire." See Ramsay to Henry Knox, 3 August 1791, Knox Family Papers, microfilm, Massachusetts Historical Society (MHS), Boston; Arthur H. Shaffer, *To Be an American: David Ramsay and the Making of American Consciousness* (Columbia: University of South Carolina Press, 1991), 165-87. Harper may have been referring to Ramsay when, at the beginning of his Cambridge oration, he spoke of a "gentleman whose learning and abilities qualify him best for expatiating on the benefits of a Liberal education, and explaining the means by which it may be promoted."

11. Harper further concluded that one of the most important aspects of education was that, unlike mere possessions, its benefits could not suddenly be taken away. On this point he anticipated the thoughts of Robert Coram and others. See Coram, *Political Inquiries: to Which is Added, a Plan for the General Establishment of Schools throughout the United States* (Wilmington: Andrews & Brynberg, 1791), reprinted in Frederick Rudolph, ed., *Essays on Education in the Early Republic* (Cambridge: Harvard University Press, 1965), 79-145; David Tyack, "Forming the National Character: Paradox in the Educational Thought of the Revolutionary Generation," *Harvard Educational Review* 36 (Winter 1966): 29-41; and Jacqueline S. Reinier, "Rearing the Republican Child: Attitudes and Practices in Post–Revolutionary Philadelphia," *William and Mary Quarterly* 39 (January 1982): 150-63.

> Can we imagine one being more superior to another than a Franklin
> a Witherspoon, or a Jefferson, to a negro just landed from the Coast
> of Africa? Yet these creatures are of the same species; they came into
> the world in all respects alike, except in the colour of their skin, and
> the difference between them, great as it appears, arises wholly from
> education. The former have received the highest cultivation of which
> human nature is capable; and they shine with the brightest rays of
> mental excellence; the latter from his infancy destitute of the least
> cultivation still grovels in the same darkness ignorance and meanness
> which accompanied him into the world.

As Harper went on to explain, varying degrees of learning, not intrinsic
levels of natural talent, created the status distinctions within society. The
"powers and advantages" of both races came not from "birth" but from
"the endowments of the mind":[12]

> Thus we see that Education, bestowing improvements on some, which
> are withheld from others, creates the vast difference we perceive in the
> degrees of mental excellence. Education sets the negro who has been
> ten years in America above him who has landed but yesterday, and
> gives him who was born among us superiority over both; education
> sets the labourer above the highest class of negroes, the man of
> business above the labourer, the gentleman of liberal education above
> both the former, and raises the Philosopher above them all.

Harper's ranking system was fraught with tensions. To a degree it
legitimated the slave trade, for a slightly educated slave was better than a
black who had "landed but yesterday." Moreover, although blacks were
theoretically capable of learning, they were not taught; thus, in reality, the
white "labourer" would always remain "above the highest class of

---

12. Unlike Harper, Thomas Jefferson believed that since Americans possessed different
levels of innate ability, educational systems had to establish procedures for the filtration
of natural talent. See Jefferson, *Notes on the State of Virginia*, edited with an introduction
by William Peden (Chapel Hill: University of North Carolina Press, 1954), 138, 162-63;
Melvin Yazawa, *From Colonies to Commonwealth: Familial Ideology and the Beginnings of
the American Republic* (Baltimore: Johns Hopkins University Press, 1985), 189;
Finkelman, "Thomas Jefferson and Anti-slavery: The Myth Goes On," *Virginia Magazine
of History and Biography* 102 (April 1994): 193-228; and generally Winthrop D. Jordan,
White over Black: American Attitudes Toward the Negro, 1550-1812 (Chapel Hill:
University of North Carolina Press, 1968), 269-311, 429-81. While Jefferson assumed that
blacks were inherently inferior to whites, Witherspoon thought both races were amenable
to the same degree of education. In 1773 he warmly supported a plan to admit "two
Negroes" to Princeton and suggested that the Quaker reformer Anthony Benezet might
help finance their education. See Witherspoon to Rev. Samuel Hopkins, 14 December
1773, MA 544, Pierpont Morgan Library (PML), New York City.

negroes." Even if blacks were to have opportunities to increase their knowledge, an unenlightened society would never accept them as full members because of their race. Perpetually degraded and with no prospects for self–improvement, slaves and free blacks were doomed to the bottom rung of the social hierarchy.

Accordingly, Harper faced a moral dilemma. Unlike his parents, who believed that sin was slavery, he had reached the conclusion that slavery was sin. By keeping blacks in a state of ignorant "darkness" where they were unable to act virtuously and embrace the "true religion," slavery, as it was practiced in South Carolina, was the temporal embodiment of evil. Although slaves appeared to have a better possibility of salvation there than in Africa, to Harper the only ethically justifiable form of bondage was one in which blacks were educated. Indeed, if his literary society were to have fulfilled its goals, it seems that this is exactly what would have occurred:

> Thus various, extensive and universal are the benefits of Learning; thus does it improve the mind, implant virtue in the heart, and promote true religion. The want of this copious, this beautiful gift among us, is acknowledged by all; all acknowledge that the means of obtaining it are rare and difficult, difficult to far the greater part, inaccessible to many. To bestow it on those to whom fortune has denied the means of obtaining it, and to render its access easier to all, are the ends for which the society, whose anniversary we now celebrate, was founded.

Unable to make a enough money to support himself in Cambridge, Harper returned to Charleston in the fall of 1789. There, he established a profitable law practice and helped train several prominent attorneys including Johnson Hagood and Samuel Gist. All the while Harper did nothing to retard the growth of slavery. With hardly a moment's hesitation, he drew up bills of sale and defended the property rights of slaveowners.[13] Though he knew no moral justification for the institution's existence, Harper rationalized its continuation. As he explained in 1787, shortly before the great compromises over slavery at the Philadelphia Convention, "Necessity indeed, that iron law, to which all others

---

13. RGH, Bill of Sale for "a Negro Man Slave named Sam," 4 June 1788, PML; General Johnson Hagood, *Meet Your Grandfather: A Sketch–Book of the Hagood–Tobin Family* (privately printed, 1946), 31-35; N. Louise Baily, *Biographical Directory of the South Carolina House of Representatives* (Columbia: University of South Carolina Press, 1984), 4: 233, 253, 261-63; and generally Terry W. Lipscomb, *South Carolina in 1791: George Washington's Southern Tour* (Columbia: South Carolina Department of Archives and History, 1993).

must submit, sometimes renders unavoidable a deviation from the maxims of Justice."[14] Since "Justice" was not the ultimate force in society, practical "Necessity" could assuage moral qualms. Regardless of the devastating ways in which slavery affected blacks, the system had to be preserved, for the prosperity of white America hung in the balance. Slaves, acknowledged Harper, were "the foundations of our wealth." Without them, the Southern economy would suffer immeasurably and the existence of liberty itself would be imperilled.[15]

Harper's awareness of the fundamental connections between slavery and freedom is vividly illustrated by his earliest surviving trial brief. In 1789, the twenty-four-year-old lawyer opposed the claims of a British loyalist who demanded compensation for a slave taken by American troops during the Revolutionary War. With a heartfelt eloquence that surely "caused tears to flow in profusion throughout the House," Harper argued that the seizure was just because it was founded on pragmatic reasons. Colonel Sumter had confiscated the "property" in order to pay his soldiers:[16]

> Murder brandished her bloody knife. Bloodshed, rapine, burning and devastation, became the sports and pastimes of our foreign enemy, and still more cruel domestic foe. The cry of infants, the dying groans of

14. Such rhetoric can be viewed as a continuing vestige of Harper's Calvinist upbringing. It is important to note, however, that he added this qualification to his statement: "but the moment that necessity ceases, interest, no less than honesty commands us to return." See RGH, "Appius's Letters to the Members of the General Assembly of the State of South Carolina: Letter One," March 1787, CTFC, MSA, SC 2360. This letter was the first of Harper's many works under the pseudonym Appius. For a less refined but printed version of the manuscript, see *The Charleston Morning Post and Daily Advertiser*, 15 & 16 February 1787.

15. At the time Harper published these remarks, he was petitioning the General Assembly for stricter debtor-relief legislation. Among other things, he worried that unscrupulous merchants might "buy in slaves at sheriff's sales and then send them to the West Indies, where they would find a ready and profitable sale." Such actions, would "ruin...the Country," but "a law to prohibit the exportation of slaves would most effectually prevent it." See Jackson Turner Main, *The Anti-federalists: Critics of the Constitution, 1783-1788* (Chapel Hill: University of North Carolina Press, 1961), 27; Jerome J. Nadelhaft, *The Disorders of War: The Revolution in South Carolina* (Orno: University of Maine at Orno Press, 1981); Staughton Lynd, *Class Conflict, Slavery, and the United States Constitution: Ten Essays* (Indianapolis: Bobbs Merrill, 1967), 153-215; and Finkelman, "Slavery and the Constitutional Convention: Making a Covenant with Death," in Richard Beeman et al., eds., *Beyond Confederation: Origins of the Constitution and American National Identity* (Chapel Hill: University of North Carolina Press, 1987), 188-225.

16. Trial Brief, 1789, HPP, MHSL; Unknown to Charles Carroll Harper, 1825, HPP, MHSL.

the aged, and the shrieks of mourning mothers, were heard throughout the land. The Sons of liberty were cut of by famine, the sword, and the halter; by open violence, or secret treachery: And the southern wing of the glorious and magnificent temple of freedom, raised by the toil, and cemented by the blood of our Country-men, shook to its lowest foundations. At this awful moment, when the expiring groans of Carolina Liberty, were now but faintly heard, Sumpter, with a Gallantry of which the history of heroic virtue affords but few examples; came to his Country's aid. He greatly resolved to alleviate her calamities, and avenge her wrongs, or yield up his life a sacrifice to her cause. But who shall second his brave attempt? Can that noble ardour which he felt be communicated to the people? can they be taught to glow with the generous flame of patriotism which lighted up his bosom? Can the love of their Country and the love of Glory draw them from their safe and peaceful retreats, to the bloody scene of hardship danger and death? No. They must be paid. Soldiers in all ages have been brought into the field by the hope of pay; and without pay no troops could then be raised.

Not only does this account powerfully reveal the limits of the Revolution's egalitarian impulses with regard to the institution of slavery; it epitomizes Edmund Morgan's contention that Americans "bought their independence with slave labor."[17] As Harper asked the judge:

After this will any one say that this slave was not taken and sold on public account, for the use of the war and with intent to give success to its operations? Not on public account, when the money arising from the sale was no otherwise disposed of but to pay the troops, who were their states only defense? Not with intent to give success to the operations of the war, when the troops who supported the war were by this very means kept in the field?

Harper's activities in the local politics of South Carolina further demonstrate his belief in the interdependence of slavery and freedom. Had he voiced the opinions from his 1788 speech on education to the slave-owning aristocrats in the state's lowcountry, they would have been

---

17. Morgan, *American Slavery-American Freedom: The American Paradox* (New York: W. W. Norton, 1975), 5. See also Duncan J. MacLeod, *Slavery, Race and the American Revolution* (Cambridge: Cambridge University Press, 1974); Sylvia R. Frey, "Liberty, Equality, and Slavery: The Paradox of the American Revolution," in Jack P. Greene, ed., *The American Revolution: Its Character and Limits* (New York: New York University Press, 1987), 230-52; and Gary B. Nash, *Race and Revolution* (Madison: Madison House, 1990).

greatly disturbed by his arguments.[18] Such utterances, however, did not bother the backcountry residents of Cambridge, though slavery was also common there. In fact, in October 1794 these voters helped elect Harper to the Fourth Congress.[19] By emphasizing racial equality in his oration, Harper had provided an ideological framework within which constituents could equate their own "political slavery" with the physical slavery of blacks.[20]

Although the white settlers in the South Carolina backcountry outnumbered those in the tidewater, the former region was greatly under-represented in the state legislature. In 1794 upcountry leaders organized the Representative Reform Association as a means of mobilizing citizens in support of reapportionment. Harper, writing under the pseudonym "Appius," became the group's leading spokesman. "In this state which calls itself free," he proclaimed in his widely circulated *Address to the People of South Carolina,* "in this state, which even glories in the name of liberty, four fifths of the people are governed by one fifth."[21]

18. They might even have attacked him personally. See Davis, *Problem of Slavery in the Age of Revolution*, 132.

19. In this same election Harper also gained a seat in the Eleventh General Assembly of the South Carolina House of Representatives. Then, in November 1794 he won a special election in the Orangeburg–Beaufort congressional district to fill the recently vacated seat of Alexander Gillon. Consequently, he served in the South Carolina legislature in the fall of 1794, qualified for the Third Congress in February 1795, and eventually took his seat as a representative of Ninety–Six district when the Fourth Congress convened later that year. See Baily, 262.

20. Comparisons between political and chattel slavery had long been prominent in South Carolina. "Whatever we may think of ourselves," declared the *South Carolina Gazette* in June 1769, "we are as real SLAVES as those we are permitted to command, and differ only in degree: for what is a slave, but one that is at the will of his master...." Quoted in Greene, "Slavery or Independence: Some Reflections on the Relationship among Liberty, Black Bondage, and Equality in Revolutionary South Carolina," *South Carolina Historical Magazine* 80 (July 1979), 202. This important article has been reprinted in idem, *Imperatives, Behaviors, and Identities: Essays in Early American Cultural History* (Charlottesville: University Press of Virginia, 1992), 268-89. See also Bernard Bailyn, *The Ideological Origins of the American Revolution* (Cambridge: Harvard University Press, 1967), 232-35; Robert M. Weir, "'The Harmony We Were Famous For': An Interpretation of Pre–Revolutionary South Carolina Politics," *William and Mary Quarterly* 26 (October 1969): 473-501; Kenneth S. Greenberg, "Revolutionary Ideology and the Proslavery Argument: The Abolition of Slavery in South Carolina," *Journal of Southern History* 42 (August 1976): 365-84; and F. Nwabueze Okoye, "Chattel Slavery as the Nightmare of the American Revolutionaries," *William and Mary Quarterly* 37 (January 1980): 3-28.

21. Pierce Butler to RGH, 4 March 1794, Butler Letterbook, 1790–1794, South Caroliniana Library (SCL), Columbia; "Appius" [RGH], *An Address to the People of South-Carolina...* (Charleston: W. P. Young, 1794), ii. Throughout July and August 1794,

(continued...)

Partly because Harper was writing in an area of the country that witnessed slavery's brutal degradations every day, his arguments found a willing and receptive audience. As the conservative Federalist Timothy Ford observed upon reading the address, "The constant example of slavery stimulates a free man to avoid being confounded with blacks; and seeing that in every instance of depression he is brought nearer to par with them, his efforts must invariably force him towards an opposite point."[22]

While under-represented upcountry farmers identified with Harper's fiery rhetoric, frightened members of the South Carolina gentry were determined to expose the potentially devastating effects of his reasoning. Henry William DeSaussure, a prominent tidewater aristocrat, maintained that if Harper's assertions about the natural equality of humanity were "adopted and reduced to practice, it would instantly free the unfortunate slaves, who form two-fifths of the whole people, and are the only cultivators of the soil in the low country."[23] Yet Appius was not in fact advocating the emancipation of South Carolina's slaves. No matter how fervently Harper rejected notions of inherent racial inferiority, he had reached the conclusion that slavery needed to exist, for without it, a huge multitude of uneducated blacks would be unleashed, jeopardizing the peace and security of society. "Our minds like our bodies, and like all the productions of nature," wrote Harper in his Cambridge address, "are weak and helpless in their infant state, but as they grow towards maturity they encrease in strength in activity and in hardiness, and their improvement in any of these particulars, is always in proportion to their exercise." The illiterate slave, never having had the proper training, was, in his opinion, simply too ignorant and debased to become a stable member of a free community.[24]

Most likely, the writings of Benjamin Rush greatly influenced this

---

21. (...continued)
Harper's address and other essays on the reapportionment controversy were published in the Charleston *City Gazette and Daily Advertiser*. For more information consult Christopher Gould and Richard Parker Morgan, *South Carolina Imprints, 1731–1800: A Descriptive Bibliography* (Santa Barbara: ABC-Clio Information Services, 1985), 223-24.

22. "Americanus" [Ford], *The Constitutionalist: or, An Inquiry How Far It is Expedient and Proper to Alter the Constitution of South-Carolina...* (Charleston: Maryland, M'Iver & Co., 1794), quoted in Greene, 204. Ford's inquiry was originally published serially during September, October, and November 1794 in the *City Gazette and Daily Advertiser*.

23. "Phocion" [DeSaussure], *Letters on the Questions of the Justice and Expediency of Going Into Alterations of the Representation in the Legislature of South Carolina...* (Charleston: Maryland and M'Iver, 1795), quoted in Greene, 206. These letters were originally published in installments during November 1794 in the *City Gazette and Daily Advertiser*.

24. RGH, "A discourse on Learning."

aspect of Harper's intellectual philosophy. "Freedom," argued Rush in his 1786 *Plan for the Establishment of Public Schools*, "can only exist in the society of knowledge." Harper agreed but contended that for America's "society of knowledge" to survive, slaves had to be excluded. The crux of the matter was this: ignorant behavior, once habitualized, became extremely difficult to alter. Lying, for example, was "generally the result of a defective education"; yet, "as a vice," it was "uncurable," just like "a disease, when it appears in adult life." Convinced that human bondage slowly deadened the moral senses of those held in captivity, Harper had essentially reworked his parents' view that some men were predestined to hell. Slaves, however, were not condemned because of an innate inferiority. Rather, since their environment prohibited them from acting in accordance with the "true religion," their subjugation became a pragmatic necessity in order to ensure the well-being of society.[25]

Despite his toleration of slavery, Harper was unable to rationalize fully his sense that the system was morally wrong and the upcountry would "be better without it." Failing to recognize this aspect of his ideology, modern historians from John Meleney to Rachel Klein have expressed bewilderment that Harper, writing as Appius, would ever have employed such divisive and threatening language during the debate over reapportionment. Klein describes Harper as utterly committed to the slave system. "Despite the fears most ably expressed by Timothy Ford and Henry William Desaussure," she concludes, "there is no evidence that any backcountry political figure ever drew anti-slavery conclusions from the rhetoric of the Revolution."[26] Harper's contemporaries certainly felt otherwise. Indeed, when Harper tried to reassure troubled slaveowners in the South Carolina lowcountry that they had nothing to fear from his arguments, he could do so only in utilitarian terms:

---

25. Rush wrote extensively on the difficulties of changing habitualized forms of behavior. Harper seems to have possessed a greater faith in the transforming power of education, but both men believed that slavery spiritually repressed blacks by suffocating their moral sense. See Rush, *An Oration Delivered Before the American Philosophical Society...* (Philadelphia: Charles Cist, 1786); idem, *A Plan for the Establishment of Public Schools and the Diffusion of Knowledge in Pennsylvania...*, reprinted in Rudolph, ed., *Essays on Education*, 1-40; Gordon S. Wood, *The Creation of the American Republic* (Chapel Hill: University of North Carolina Press, 1969), 46-90; Yazawa, 162; and RGH, "A discourse on Learning."

26. "Appius" [RGH], *An Address*, 21; Meleney, *The Public Life of Aedanus Burke: Revolutionary Republican in Post-Revolutionary South Carolina* (Columbia: University of South Carolina Press, 1989), 217-19; and Klein, *Unification of a Slave State: The Rise of the Planter Class in the South Carolina Backcountry, 1760-1808* (Chapel Hill: University of North Carolina Press, 1990), 150, 177, 221-28, 275.

You have been told, fellow citizens, that should we succeed in our plan of reform, the next step would be to lay enormous taxes on your property, and perhaps to liberate your slaves. But look at the census and you will find that we too have slaves, though not as many as you. There is not one member of the middle and western districts who is not a slave owner....Should any member from that part of the State propose the abolition of slavery, which however, considering that they are all slave–owners themselves, is surely not to be apprehended, there can be no doubt that he would be tarred and feathered as soon as he returned home.[27]

The objections of Klein and other scholars notwithstanding, the Representative Reform Association's efforts were defeated during the winter of 1794–95 largely because the tidewater elite had good reason to believe that "Appian" assumptions fundamentally challenged the moral underpinnings of slavery, and, if left unchecked, might spawn a still more radical, abolitionist critique. In addition to propagating controversial political and educational beliefs, Harper had long articulated a vision of regional development far different from that of other leaders within the state. From 1791 to 1795 numerous speculative schemes, including what would eventually become known as the Yazoo land frauds, left him deeply in debt. Still, he continued to acquire vast amounts of acreage in western Georgia and South Carolina.[28] It was his dream for pious and industrious New England families someday "to remove there, take their clergy-men & school-masters, their smiths carpenters, & masons with them & form a town." While this plan would be financially advantageous for both parties, Harper anticipated that one of the greatest benefits would be to the white settlers already living in the backcountry, whom he considered nearly as degraded as slaves. Harper hoped that in due course the "good citizens" from the North "would set them the example of industry & economy, instruct them in agriculture, & furnish a model of an excellent internal police, by which the whole Country might gradually

27. RGH, "An Address From the Representatives of the People in the Middle And Western Districts, Met at Columbia, December 17, 1794, to their Fellow–Citizens in the Eastern Parts of the State," *City Gazette and Daily Advertiser*, 29 October 1795.

28. For more information on Harper's activities as a speculator and eventually as a lawyer for John Peck, see RGH, Autobiography, HPP, MHSL; *An Extract from the Proceedings of the South–Carolina Yazoo Company* (Charleston: A. Timothy, 1791); RGH, *The Case of the Georgia Sales on the Mississippi...* (Philadelphia: Richard Folwell for Benjamin Davies, 1797); Ronald Edward Bridwell, "The South's Wealthiest Planter: Wade Hampton I of South Carolina, 1754–1835" (Ph.D. Dissertation, University of South Carolina, 1980); and C. Peter Magrath, *Yazoo: Law and Politics in the New Republic* (Providence: Brown University Press, 1966).

be formed into similar institutions."[29]

Harper's plan for settling the frontier challenged the assumptions of tidewater aristocrats in two important ways. First, it advanced the radical notion that slavery's westward expansion was neither desirable nor essential for the state's future prosperity. Second, it suggested that if given the proper training, backcountry settlers could become free and equal citizens. Though Harper admitted that some degree of inequity would always exist between residents of the upcountry and the lowcountry, he insisted that this imbalance should never be society's goal. In his opinion the purpose of local and federal government was to ensure the natural rights of individuals so that each would have the opportunity to maximize his innate moral potential. As he explained during the debate over reapportionment:

> [E]quality is the natural condition of man; the basis of his moral excellence, and political happiness....[A]lthough "*equality of conditions*" cannot be preserved in society, "*equality of rights*" is not only consistent with good government, but forms its only firm and lasting foundation....[T]o suffer property to be directly represented, would destroy this equality, by giving rich men different and more numerous political rights than their neighbors, whose masters they would thus become.[30]

Prominent members of the South Carolina gentry responded to Harper's assertions by emphasizing the importance of social distinctions based upon wealth, connections, and ability. "[I]nequality," wrote Thomas Tudor Tucker, "so far from being an evil, is absolutely necessary to the well being of society; it is the cement that binds together the various employments of life, and forms the whole into a beautiful system of mutual dependencies." According to Tucker, social leveling not only bred "ignorance" by stifling man's desire for self-improvement, but because individuals were born with differing capacities for certain skills, it also worked to retard God's will. Some men, reasoned Tucker, "have more strength than others, some more industry, and some more ingenuity....[A]ccording to these, and many other circumstances, the products of their labour must be various, and their property must become unequal."[31]

In Harper's judgment the majority of such differences resulted from

---

29. RGH to Col. Wadsworth, 27 October 1795, Boston Public Library (BPL).

30. "Appius" [RGH], *An Address*, iii.

31. Tucker, *An Oration Delivered in St. Michael's Church...on the 4th of July, 1795...* (Charleston: Timothy and Mason, 1795), quoted in Meleney, 271-72.

education, not birthright:

> A person who from infancy to manhood has been accustomed to lift great weights, and to spend much of his time in laborious employments, will possess far greater strength, and be much more capable of sustaining fatigues and hardship, than one who has spent his life in idleness or in sedentary occupations. Take two young horses of equal blood and equal beauty, let one be exercised in leaping and running; neglect the other, or employ him in drawing a cart, and how greatly will the former excell in swiftness and agility? Thus also the infant mind is improved by exercise and that exercise learning supplies.

Of course, certain examples seemed "to contradict this opinion." While some men were naturally brilliant, others had trouble learning even after "much care" had been "employed." Yet, as Harper repeatedly insisted, exposure to learning was by far the most influential factor in determining one's status: "If the man who without the aid of mental improvement has obtained distinction by the...inborn force of his genius, had enjoyed the advantages which learning can bestow, how much more illustrious would his talents have appeared! on the other hand had he whom not education itself could rescue from ignorance and dulness, been deprived of that help, into what gulph of stupidity must [he] have sunk!"[32]

The ways in which Harper attempted to mobilize backcountry residents during the debate over reapportionment symbolically reflect this mind-set. Assuming the role of pedagogue, as he would continue to do throughout his life, he kept his constituents continually informed by publishing detailed explanations of his reasoning.[33] Harper never doubted that to achieve his objectives, he needed only to fashion appeals based on logic and common sense. "For we have too much reliance," wrote Harper as Appius, "on the justice, the patriotism, and the prudence of those who compose the legislature of this country, to believe that they will, on any occasion, much less on one of such importance as this, shut their ears to the well founded and general complaints of their constituents and fellow

---

32. RGH, "A discourse on Learning."

33. During his time in Congress, Harper published far more letters to his constituents than any other representative. These long and detailed reports have been collected in the first volume of Noble E. Cunningham, Jr., *Circular Letters of Congressmen to Their Constituents*, 3 vols. (Chapel Hill: University of North Carolina Press, 1978). For an older but easy-to-find edition see Elizabeth Donnan, "The Papers of James A. Bayard, 1796–1815," *Annual Report of the American Historical Association for the Year 1913* (Washington: Government Printing Office, 1915).

citizens, when properly expressed and made known to them."[34]

Ironically, as the 1790's passed, it was Harper's faith in education that would eventually pose the greatest challenge to his vision. If slaves could be educated to the same degree as whites, it only stood to reason that the more they learned of freedom, the sooner they would claim independence for themselves by taking up arms against their former masters.

---

34. "Appius" [RGH], *An Address*, vi.

CHAPTER TWO

The Burning Fuse:
Revolution and the Coming of the Apocalypse

A S WORD OF THE FRENCH Revolution reached the United States,
Robert Goodloe Harper received the news with great "joy" and "exultation." To the young lawyer, liberty, equality, and the "true rights of man" seemed to be spreading throughout the world. In October 1793, when most Republicans had begun to distance themselves from the embarrassing behavior of Citizen Edmond Charles Genet, Harper became the Vice President of Charleston's radical Jacobin Club. Donning a tricolor cockade, he proudly strolled the city's streets, likely humming "La Marseillaise" and embracing those he passed.[1] "While France appeared to be engaged in a struggle for liberty and national independence," Harper later wrote, "no heart beat higher than mine with affection for her cause":[2]

> I joined with enthusiasm in the general exultation of my country for
> her victories, mourned her disasters, and wished to draw a veil over
> her crimes, her follies, and her excesses. Even her crimes appeared
> only as mistakes in my eyes, and her most enormous atrocities as nat-
> ural, and perhaps necessary consequences of the violent external and
> internal struggles wherein she was engaged: I called them the crimes
> of the revolution, not of France, and I pardoned them. Where I could
> not pardon, I excused them, I palliated. I considered her as fighting in
> the cause of freedom and humanity, and an end so excellent afforded
> much consolation for the means which she often employed.

---

1. RGH to the Philadelphia *National Gazette*, 15 December 1824, HPP, MHSL; *Annals of Congress*, 5th Congress, 2nd Session, 1354-55; Michael L. Kennedy, "A French Jacobin Club in Charleston, South Carolina, 1792-1795," *South Carolina Historical Magazine* 91 (January 1990): 4-21; Philadelphia *Aurora*, 21 March 1797; Harry Ammon, *The Genet Mission* (New York: W. W. Norton, 1973); E. S. Thomas, *Reminiscences of the Last Sixty-Five Years...*, 2 vols. (Hartford: Case, Tiffany, & Burnham, 1840), 1: 32-33; and Charles Fraser, *Reminiscences of Charleston...* (Charleston: John Russell, 1854), 42-43.

2. RGH, *Observations on the Dispute Between the United States and France* (Philadelphia, 1797), 5-6. This pamphlet was extremely popular and was reprinted at least seven times in the United States and fourteen times in Britain. It also was translated into French and Portuguese.

Harper's zealous Francophilia eventually subsided. The Revolution he at first heralded as a "blessing to the world" soon became "the greatest curse that ever afflicted mankind...a phial of wrath from Heaven, the bitterest that ever was poured out upon the earth." Historians have suggested two possible explanations for this abrupt metamorphosis. David Hackett Fischer maintains that Harper's original support for the French Revolution derived from his personal insecurities and inner longing for "social acceptance." Since "group approval was the goal of his vague and powerful ambition," Harper simply switched sides once backing France was no longer advantageous. Unlike Fischer, Joseph Cox contends that Harper in fact never fully embraced the French Revolution. Interpretations that suggest Harper did so, according to Cox, are little more than the self-serving propaganda of "Jeffersonian inclined" scholars hoping to characterize Harper "as the classic prototype of opportunistic, militant, and nativistic Federalism."[3]

While Cox's conclusions are contradicted by the existing evidence, Fischer's analysis only begins to decipher Harper's complex psychology. As we have already seen, Harper subjected his vision of spiritual redemption to the practical limitations of society. Mankind was its own moral guardian, but with this stewardship came the cumbersome responsibility of reconciling idyllic hopes of a better existence with worldly imperfection. In Harper's mind, America was perched precariously "between the two extremes of Anarchy on the one hand and Slavery on the other." Education provided the knowledge and virtue necessary to "fine-tune" this equilibrium, but mankind's journey from Egypt to the Promised Land would be long and difficult. As the political theorist Michael Walzer has observed, for those, like Harper, who understood humanity's progress according to an "Exodus paradigm," effecting change required years of "marching across the desert, teaching, learning, [and] obeying the law."[4]

---

3. *Annals of Congress*, 5th Congress, 2nd Session, 1355; Fischer, "Robert Goodloe Harper" (Senior Thesis, Princeton University, 1958), 19-21; and Cox, 30-32, 40-45.

4. RGH, "Appius's Letters to the Members of the General Assembly of the State of South Carolina: Letter One," March 1787, CTFC, MSA; Walzer, *Exodus and Revolution* (New York: Basic Books, 1985), 130-49. For Harper's numerous references to defending the "balance" within society, see Fischer, "Robert Goodloe Harper," 30-31, 76-111. As Davis explains, "[T]he tension between millennial perfection and present reality requires constant readjustment or tuning....If the tension becomes too great, as on a cello, the
(continued...)

The millennialist spirit of the 1790s threatened to upset the delicate balance of Harper's world. An increasing desire to "force the end" generated an apocalyptic mentality that ignored the constraints of temporal reality. Traditional conceptions of evil were redefined, and sin itself became justified as a means of obtaining salvation. As Jefferson wrote in 1793:

> The liberty of the whole earth was depending on the issue of the contest, and was ever such a prize won with so little innocent blood? My own affections have been deeply wounded by some of the martyrs to this cause, but rather than it should have failed I would have seen half the earth desolated; were there but an Adam and Eve left in every country, and left free, it would be better than as it now is.

Unwilling to have his universe shaken, Harper recoiled in horror as tales of the Terror's mass destruction reached the United States. The chaotic forces of Revolution promised to undermine the social order and thus "pull down a stupendous fabric." Bondage, not liberation, would be the result as mankind plunged backward toward anarchy and violence.[5]

More than any other factor, it was the South's preponderance of slaves that convinced Harper to forsake his earlier ardor for the French cause. In all nations, he observed, "the army of revolution...is composed

---

4.(...continued)
bridge bends backward and the strings finally snap. This is the familiar situation when revolutionaries approve the annihilation of any present reality in the pursuit of a messianic ideal....But if the better world seems too remote or chimerical, or if apologists succeed in idealizing the present order, the cello strings slacken until complacent flat notes give way to silence." It is interesting to note that Harper's opponents mockingly referred to him as a "Harp" with great "versatility." In their estimation "the instrument" was of "a superior excellence," for it constantly changed tunes. See Davis, *Revolutions: Reflections on American Equality and Foreign Liberations* (Cambridge: Harvard University Press, 1990), 23-24; *Aurora*, 30 March 1796.

5. Nash, "The American Clergy and the French Revolution," *William and Mary Quarterly* 22 (July 1965): 392-412; John R. Howe, Jr., "Republican Thought and the Political Violence of the 1790s," *American Quarterly* 19 (Summer 1967): 147-65; Nathan O. Hatch, *The Sacred Cause of Liberty: Republican Thought and the Millennium in Revolutionary New England* (New Haven: Yale University Press, 1977), 97-138; Ruth Bloch, *Visionary Republic: Millennial Themes in American Thought, 1756-1800* (Cambridge: Cambridge University Press, 1985), 202-21; Davis, *Revolutions*, 47; Jefferson to William Short, 3 January 1793, in Andrew A. Lipscomb, ed., *The Writings of Thomas Jefferson*, 20 vols. (Washington: Thomas Jefferson Memorial Association, 1903-1904), 9: 10; and *Annals of Congress*, 5th Congress, 2nd Session, 1177.

of the *sans-culottes*, that class of idle, indigent, and profligate persons, who so greatly abound in the populous countries of Europe, especially the large towns; and being destitute of everything, having no home, no family, no regular means of subsistence, feel no attachment to the established order, which they are always ready to join in subverting, when they find one to pay them for their assistance." "[F]ortunately for America," continued Harper:

> there are few *sans-culottes* among her inhabitants, very few indeed. Except some small portions of rabble in a few towns, the character is unknown among us; and hence our safety. Our people are all, or very nearly all, proprietors of land, spread over a vast extent of country, where they live in ease and freedom; strangers alike to oppression and want.

Though most citizens had no reason to revolt, Harper realized that slavery engendered "a certain class of men" who would emotionally and materially benefit from social upheaval. Accordingly, he faced an intolerable paradox. On the one hand, American freedom depended upon the subordination of a servile race, for slaves, by performing society's most menial tasks, prevented a class of white "*sans-culottes*" from developing. At the same time, however, black dissatisfaction with the resulting hierarchy threatened to destroy the very structure their labor made possible.[6]

The bloody uprisings in Saint Domingue confirmed Harper's deep anxieties that America's slave population might soon become a dangerous "army of revolution." Shortly after word of the rebellion reached the United States in September 1791, South Carolina's Governor, Charles Pinckney, wrote to the colony's assembly:

> When we recollect how nearly similar the situation of the Southern States and St. Domingo are in the profusion of slaves—that a day may arrive when they may be exposed to the same insurrections—we cannot but sensibly feel for your situation.

Two years later, when a French fleet arrived with nearly 10,000 white refugees and their slaves, Southerners greeted the West Indian aristocrats

---

6. *Annals of Congress*, 5th Congress, 2nd Session, 1179, 1530-31; Morgan, 295-315.

with a massive outpouring of "charity and affection." Yet, as accounts of
the devastation and racial violence in Saint Domingue spread throughout
the country, many South Carolinians began to fear that their own slaves
were in danger of being "contaminated." In October 1793 Charleston
authorities passed a resolution stating that "any vessel...from St. Domingo
with passengers, Negroes or people of color shall remain under the guns
of Ft. Johnson till such passengers as the committee may deem improper
to admit, and the Negroes and people of color be sent out of the state."
That same month, *The New York Journal and Patriotic Register* reported:[7]

> They write from Charleston...that the NEGROES have become very
> insolent, in so much that the citizens are alarmed, and the militia keep
> a constant guard. It is said that the Santo Domingo Negroes have
> sown those seeds of revolt, and that a magazine has been attempted
> to be broken open.

Tensions increased still further in February 1794 when the French
National Convention abolished slavery. "We are to have a meeting of the
citizens," wrote Nathaniel Russell from Charleston, "...when I hope some
effective measure will be adopted to prevent any evil consequences from
that diabolical decree of the national convention which emancipates all
the slaves in the french colonies, a circumstance the most alarming that
could happen to this country." One of the possibilities discussed at that
gathering was to "expel from the state all Negroes without exception that
have within the last three years arrived here from the French West India
Islands." During the summer of 1794 this motion gathered support
throughout South Carolina. In the Columbia *Herald*, "Rusticus" not
only advocated the forcible removal of all French blacks but also insisted
that "self-preservation" made it incumbent upon the state's many

---

7. Thomas O. Ott, *The Haitian Revolution, 1789-1804* (Knoxville: University of Tennessee
Press, 1973), 53; George D. Terry, "A Study of the Impact of the French Revolution and
the Insurrections in Saint-Domingue upon South Carolina, 1790-1805" (Master's Thesis,
University of South Carolina, 1975); Donald R. Hickey, "America's Response to the Slave
Revolt in Haiti, 1791-1806," *Journal of the Early Republic* 2 (Winter 1982): 361-79; Michael
Zuckerman, "The Power of Blackness: Thomas Jefferson and the Revolution in St.
Domingue," *Almost Chosen People: Oblique Biographies in the American Grain* (Berkeley:
University of California Press, 1993), 175-218; Eric Robert Papenfuse, "From Recompense
to Revolution: *Mahoney v. Ashton* and the Transfiguration of Maryland Culture, 1791-
1802," *Slavery and Abolition* 15 (December 1994): 38-62; David Patrick Geggus, *Slavery,
War, and Revolution: The British Occupation of Saint-Domingue, 1793-1798* (Oxford:
Clarendon Press, 1982), 110, 305; and Jordan, 381.

newspapers to limit the scope of their reports on events in Saint Domingue.[8]

Amid this frenzied atmosphere Harper determined to run for public office. Intent on effecting change within the bounds of civil society, he saw politics as the most rational and pragmatic way to implement his vision. Yet by the time he arrived in Congress, an American slave insurrection loomed so ominously on the horizon that the newly elected representative could no longer sustain his earlier optimism. As DeSaussure reminded him, pronouncements like "equality is the natural condition of man," which Harper had made during the debate over reapportionment, were now more dangerous than ever. Their adoption "would ruin the country, by giving liberty to the slaves, and desolating the land with fire and sword in the struggles between master and slave: a fate which has attended the French West India Islands from the too hasty adoption of these axioms in all their extent."[9]

All this was too much for Harper to endure. Could it be that in Cambridge he had been a philosopher, one of those "pioneers of revolution" who "talk of the perfectibility of man, of the dignity of his nature; and entirely forgetting what he is, declaim perpetually about what he should be"? Of course not, he assured himself. Such men "advance always in front, and prepare the way, by preaching infidelity, and weakening the respect of the people for ancient institutions." He had never meant to challenge the fundamental order of society. Could it be that he had once consorted with Jacobins, those "worthless scoundrels and mad-headed enthusiasts, who, in endeavoring to reduce their fallacious schemes to practice, have introduced more calamities into the world than ages of good government will be able to cure"? Certainly not! As he explained before Congress, in the early 1790s he had attended one or two meetings of Charleston's Patriotic Society, but what had been said "respecting his being a member of a Jacobin society is one of those falsehoods of party, which, though known to be unfounded, is still

---

8. Nathaniel Russell to Ralph Izard, 6 June 1794, quoted in Ulrich B. Phillips, "The South Carolina Federalists," *American Historical Review* 14 (1909), 735; "Rusticus" [Alexander Garden, Jr.], Columbia *Herald*, 14 July 1794, quoted in Alfred N. Hunt, *Haiti's Influence on Antebellum America: Slumbering Volcano in the Caribbean* (Baton Rouge: Louisiana State University Press, 1988), 111.

9. Alexander Gillon to Wade Hampton, 20 January 1793, Hampton Family Papers, SCL; "Phocion" [DeSaussure], *Letters on the Question*, 29-30, quoted in Klein, 226-27.

reported."[10]

Harper was deceiving himself, and many prominent South Carolinians recognized it. Pierce Butler, for example, "despised" Harper for having deserted the Republican party. Writing to Aedanus Burke in the summer of 1796, he bemoaned Harper's conversion to Federalism and insisted that "the less we have to do with so unprincipled a man the better."[11] Burke also detested Harper for having "bolted the moment he started from the post." In two open letters "To Caroliniensis, alias Mr. H---R, a delegate in Congress," first published in January and March 1796, Burke reminded readers of the *South Carolina State Gazette* that Harper, when writing as Appius, had accused tidewater aristocrats of being steadfastly "determined to make the upper country a sort of a land of Egypt, and a house of Bondage":[12]

> But I had like to have forgotten, that you were then a good democrat and sans–cullote, who hated aristocrats, and whose duty it was *to low jealousies*, and cry down aristocracy and its adherents: in short, to enflame men's minds against this same government, which now you pretend to support. Again, you had to mix with the people of the interior country, to cajole and manoeuver your gay and beauish broad–cloth dress, being aristocratic, you laid it aside and in deception of a republican, patriotic people, you sir, in all the sincerity of your humble sans–cullote spirit, you dressed yourself from head to foot in back–country homespun manufacture, and returning to town, you again became the petit–maitre! This was not all, your very stomach and appetite, it seems, turned democratic: whiskey, you said, was the true genuine drink of a democrat: as to madeira wine, you left it to the aristocrats of Charleston. That you condescended to these and some other mean artifices, which I decline to mention, is universally reported, and there is no question that the judicious part of your constituents are now ashamed of having been duped by it.

While Republicans such as Burke condemned Harper for "prostitut-

10. *Annals of Congress*, 5th Congress, 2nd Session, 1178-79, 1354.

11. Butler to Burke, 31 March & 7 June 1796, Butler Letterbook, 1794-1822, Historical Society of Pennsylvania (HSP), Philadelphia.

12. *South Carolina State Gazette*, 8 January & 5 March 1796, cited in Meleney, 226-34. I would like to thank Conyers Bull of the Charleston Library Society for graciously providing me with transcripts of Burke's letters.

ing his sincerity" in order to achieve "his main object, that is helping himself," other writers insisted that the motives of "the incendiary of Ninety-Six" were far more sinister. According to James T. Callendar, Harper's support for the Jay Treaty and similar Francophobic policies was so unjustified that it "cast Nero and his conflagration into the shade." Indeed, these measures amounted to "robbery more unprovoked, more shameless, more criminal...[than had ever been] suggested in the cabin of Blackbeard, or the camp of Brandt."[13] Most Federalists, on the other hand, expressed delight at Harper's change in attitude. In 1794 Ralph Izard had accused the Representative of laying "the foundation for greater trouble in So Carolina" by advocating plans that would "inevitably destroy security of Property and Government." Yet by 1798 Izard was writing to Jacob Read, "I approve very much of the conduct of Mr. Harper, & regret extremely that a person capable of behaving so well should have done so much mischief by the publication of the Letters of Appius."[14]

 Having converted to Federalism, Harper quickly rose to prominence as the powerful chairman of the House Ways and Means Committee. It was in this capacity that he is believed to have uttered the famous words, "Millions for defense, but not a cent for tribute!" Modern historians have interpreted this remark within the context of the XYZ affair and escalating tensions with France. Few scholars, however, have drawn attention to what Harper at the time believed the greatest threat to national security.[15] In April 1798, acting on information supplied to him by Secretary of State Timothy Pickering, Harper rose before Congress to

13. Callendar, *Sketches of the History of America* (Philadelphia: Snowden & M'Corkle, 1798), 52, 256. For Harper's support of the Jay Treaty, see RGH, *An Address from Robert Goodloe Harper, of South Carolina, to His Constituents, Containing His Reasons for Approving the Treaty of Amity, Commerce, and Navigation, with Great Britain* (Philadelphia: Ormrod and Conrad, 1795); "Caroliniensis" [RGH], *South Carolina State Gazette*, 7 January 1796; *Annals of Congress*, 4th Congress, 1st Session, 457-64; RGH, *Observations*; Harper's circular letters collected in Cunningham; and George C. Rogers, Jr., *Evolution of a Federalist: William Loughton Smith of Charleston (1758-1812)* (Columbia: University of South Carolina Press, 1962).

14. Izard to Mathias Hutchinson, 1794, quoted in Klein, 227; Izard to Read, 9 May 1798, Ralph Izard Papers, SCL.

15. A. S. Salley, Jr., ed., "Notes and Queries," *South Carolina Historical and Genealogical Magazine* 1 (1900): 100-103; Samuel Eliot Morison, *Harrison Gray Otis, 1765-1848: The Urbane Federalist* (Boston: Houghton Mifflin, 1969), 113; and Thomas M. Ray, "'Not One Cent for Tribute': The Public Addresses and American Popular Reaction to the XYZ Affair, 1798-99," *Journal of the Early Republic* 3 (Winter 1983): 389-412.

FIGURE TWO. Harper at the height of his political power. Charcoal and white chalk on paper by Charles Balthazar Julien Févret de Saint–Mémin, 1799. Courtesy of the Maryland Historical Society.

warn that five thousand "black troops" were preparing to invade the United States from Saint Domingue. These forces, he alleged, were "within four or five days sail." Not only were they plotting to turn Southern slaves against their masters, but unless the nation raised an "effective force" to resist their assault "whenever wherever it may show its head," the impending alliance between American slaves and French blacks would "destroy the country."[16]

The following month Harper again implored the House to authorize greater expenditures for defense. The South, he claimed, was too "exposed" to defend against invasion:[17]

> We know...that Victor Hugues and Toussaint have each of them considerable force, and though not sufficient, perhaps, to expel the troops from St. Domingo, they might be sufficient to send against our Southern coast, and do considerable damage before any opposition could be made to them....[We also know] that the black population on the seacoast is very great, and that there is a large tract of country full of fastnesses and marshes between them and the white population, and that if the blacks once made a lodgement in these marshes, it would be difficult to drive them off.

This fantastic plan never materialized. Yet almost a year later, Harper was unwilling to admit that he had been wrong. "Last summer," he explained in a circular letter to his constituents, "...Hedouville, was preparing to invade the southern states from St. Domingo, with an army of blacks, which was to be landed with a large supply of officers, arms and ammunition to excite an insurrection among the negroes, by means of emissaries previously sent, and first to subjugate the country by their assistance, and then plunder and lay it waste." To support his conten-

16. Pickering to Harper, 21 March 1798, cited in Alexander DeConde, *The Quasi-War: The Politics and Diplomacy of the Undeclared War with France, 1797-1801* (New York: Charles Scribner's Sons, 1966), 84; James D. Essig, *The Bonds of Wickedness: American Evangelicals Against Slavery, 1770-1808* (Philadelphia: Temple University Press, 1982), 126-27; Stanley Elkins and Eric McKitrick, *The Age of Federalism* (New York: Oxford University Press, 1993), 598; and *Annals of Congress*, 5th Congress, 2nd Session, 1530-31.

17. Historians Ronald Hatzenbuehler and Robert Ivie use Harper's rhetoric to support their conclusion that he and other Federalist War Hawks "never articulated a threatening image of French attacks." Amazingly, however, their study fails to mention the problem of slave insurrection. See Hatzenbuehler and Ivie, *Congress Declares War: Rhetoric, Leadership, and Partisanship in the Early Republic* (Kent, Ohio: Kent State University Press, 1983), 65-72; *Annals of Congress*, 5th Congress, 2nd Session, 1647.

tions, Harper stubbornly relied on dubious sources. One Kentucky reader angrily responded:[18]

> From your want of success in establishing by sufficient proof, any of the numberless plots which you had before this detected, and promised to prove the existence of; as well your declaration that your assertions as to this scheme, were founded "on the most accurate and undoubted information," I concluded, that I should immediately see the most conclusive evidence, of the existence of this scheme: but my astonishment was great indeed, when I found, that the only proof, that you adduced, to support it, was, *your assertion*, that you had had the story, "from a person of the highest confidence, *who had had it* from a man of honor and character here, *who had been sent* by a merchant of Philadelphia to St. Domingo, and who while there conversed with some of the *black officers*, who were to be employed in the expedition, and who, as he spoke their language well, he was led to cultivate an acquaintance with, and from them in their moments of conviviality, he learned the project."

This unabashed willingness to cite questionable authorities illustrates the extent of Harper's paranoid style.[19] The threat seemed so real and the stakes so high that the skilled and methodical lawyer was willing to base his entire case upon hearsay.[20] Although he genuinely believed that a

---

18. It is important to note Harper's willingness to embrace the word of "black officers." Despite his heightened fears, he continued to believe that blacks could be both educated and relied on. In fact, it was this very realization which made the prospect of black revolution so vivid in his mind. See RGH to his constituents, 20 March 1799, in Cunningham, 163-74; *Correspondence Between George Nicholas, Esq. of Kentucky, and The Hon. Robert G. Harper, Member of Congress from the District of 96, State of South Carolina* (Lexington: John Bradford, 1799), 20-21.

19. I use the term "paranoid" carefully. As the historian Richard Hofstadter has urged, it should not be construed in the clinical sense. Underneath all of Harper's endeavors lay a fundamental conviction that a great threat was "directed against a nation, a culture, [and] a way of life." See Hofstadter, "The Paranoid Style in American Politics," in Davis, ed., *The Fear of Conspiracy: Images of Un–American Subversion from the Revolution to the Present* (Ithaca: Cornell University Press, 1971), 2-9; Wood, "Conspiracy and the Paranoid Style: Causality and Deceit in the Eighteenth Century," *William and Mary Quarterly* 39 (July 1982): 401-41; and Hutson, "The Origins of 'The Paranoid Style in American Politics': Public Jealousy from the Age of Walpole to the Age of Jackson," in David D. Hall, John M. Murrin, and Thad W. Tate, eds., *Saints and Revolutionaries: Essays on Early American History* (New York: W. W. Norton, 1984), 332-72.

20. The threat was "real" only in Harper's mind. Toussaint was preoccupied with
(continued...)

slave insurrection was imminent, Harper's fears also masked a deeper self–deception. Lacking moral grounds for tolerating slavery's existence, he let himself believe that a black revolution was spreading to the United States; such fears reinforced the institution's "necessity" and assured him of the importance of national unity. Despite Harper's philosophical commitment to the widespread dissemination of knowledge, the specter of rebellion offered a convenient means of deflecting his inner anxieties about educating blacks while rationalizing his support for restrictive legislation such as the Alien and Sedition Acts.[21]

The kinds of speech Harper found most objectionable were strident ideological arguments that might expose the tensions he had so uneasily accommodated in his mind. In November 1797 Harper opposed the second reading of a Quaker petition decrying the "wrongs and cruelties practiced upon the poor African race" and calling for an end to the slave trade. These pronouncements, he argued, "had a tendency to stir up a class of persons to inflict calamities which would be of greater consequence than any evils which were at present suffered; and this, and every other Legislature, ought to set their faces against remonstrances complaining of what it was utterly impossible to alter." For many Quakers slavery was a hideous atrocity, blocking the way to redemption. "American

---

20.(...continued)
domestic problems and never intended to invade the United States. When the French ordered an attack on Jamaica in 1798, he refused to comply. See "Letters of Toussaint Louverture to Edward Stevens, 1798-1800," *American Historical Review* 16 (October 1910): 64-101. Harper's conspiracy theories were mocked in the Republican press. See especially the Boston *Independent Chronicle*, 18 March 1799, cited in Donald Stewart, *The Opposition Press of the Federalist Period* (Albany: New York University Press, 1969), 326; James Tagg, *Benjamin Franklin Bache and the Philadelphia Aurora* (Philadelphia: University of Pennsylvania Press, 1991); and Alexandra Lee Levin, "James Buchanan's Letters from Baltimore, 1798,"*Maryland Historical Magazine* 74 (December 1979): 344-57.

21. For general and often critical accounts of Harper's role in framing the Alien and Sedition Acts as well as impeaching Senator William Blount, see Manning J. Dauer, *The Adams Federalists* (Baltimore: Johns Hopkins Press, 1953); Morton Borden, *The Federalism of James A. Bayard* (New York: Columbia University Press, 1955); James Morton Smith, *Freedom's Fetters: The Alien and Sedition Laws and American Civil Liberties* (Ithaca: Cornell University Press, 1956); George S. McCowen, Jr., "The Broad Constructionist Views of William Loughton Smith and Robert Goodloe Harper" (Master's Thesis, Emory University, 1957); Hofstadter, *The Idea of a Party System: The Rise of Legitimate Opposition in the United States, 1780-1840* (Berkeley: University of California Press, 1969); Richard Buel, Jr., *Securing the Revolution: Ideology in American Politics, 1789-1815* (Ithaca: Cornell University Press, 1972); and Peter Charles Hoffer and N. E. H. Hull, *Impeachment in America, 1635-1805* (New Haven: Yale University Press, 1984).

slavery," observes the historian David Brion Davis, "was the Antichrist and the seven-headed dragon of Revelation. The Lord was whetting his glittering sword, and his vengeance was certain, unless the new Children of Israel separated themselves from the filthiness of the Heathen, and came away from Babylon." Unlike the Quakers, Harper had come to view slavery as an evil necessity on which the freedom of the United States rested. If the "dragon" were at the door, so to speak, it became all the more important not to let him in. "Fanatics" like the Society of Friends who refused to accept the limits of reality were themselves vicious harbingers of Armageddon.[22]

Still, on one level Harper could identify with the Quakers. Their motives were "pure," and their actions were "well-intentioned," but despite such "good intentions," emancipation would have "direful" consequences. It would only foster a grim parody of interracial union, the grotesque mingling of "blood and bones" upon a war-torn battle-field:[23]

> Do we not confine lunatics and keep knives and razors out of the hands of children? Why? Not because we are afraid of their intentions, but of their actions; because we are justly apprehensive of their doing mischief without intending it. Is there a description of a people on earth, who have inspired the world with a firmer confidence in their good intentions than the Quakers? And yet we dread the consequences of some of their attempts. This society, so virtuous, so praiseworthy, and whose institutions are formed on principles so beneficial and benevolent, have, however, adopted it as part of their creed, have made it a tenet of their religion, that personal slavery ought to be abolished; and they go forward with unwearied perseverance to the accomplishment of this object, without regard to the risks or consequences. In vain do we tell them that their attempts, if successful, must render the Southern States a new St. Domingo—a mournful scene of massacre, pillage, and conflagration—must end in the common destruction of the blacks and whites, the slaves and their masters. In vain do we hold up to their view the recent and neighbor-

---

22. *Annals of Congress*, 5th Congress, 2nd Session, 657-658; Davis, *Problem of Slavery in Western Culture*, 326; James Roger Sharp, *American Politics in the Early Republic: The New Nation in Crisis* (New Haven: Yale University Press, 1993), 176; and generally Merton Lynn Dillon, *Slavery Attacked: Southern Slaves and their Allies, 1619-1865* (Baton Rouge: Louisiana State University Press, 1990).

23. *Annals of Congress*, 5th Congress, 2nd Session, 1176.

ing example of the French Islands, where similar maxims have reduced the most flourishing and beautiful provinces to one great slaughterpen—have everywhere mingled the blood and bones of the wretched inhabitants with the ashes of their dwellings. They answer, that they have no intention to produce these consequences, and do not apprehend them; that it is their duty to proceed, and that the consequences are with God.

In many respects, the Quakers, by attempting to do all that Harper wanted to do but could not, represent his liberated conscience. Since Harper thought slavery was both a moral evil and a practical necessity, he could praise Quaker intentions but never their actions, even though the group's philanthropic endeavors were often in keeping with his educational philosophy. Just two years after Harper's Cambridge oration, a young black girl in Pennsylvania wrote to her Quaker benefactors:[24]

> Esteemed friends I am lead by a humble Sense of Gratitude and duty to return you most affectionate acknowledgments for the kind attention you have condescended towards the improvement of our useful Learning as well as the inculcating us in the more excellent precepts that of our Religious duties. [I] earnestly trust [that you] will be Blessed in the ardent endeavors to persevere for that promotion which will afford a comfortable satisfaction, to you, and a lasting happiness to ourselves....

This black student had been taught to read, write, and express herself as well as any white child. While the Quakers were willing to attempt such projects, Harper, enslaved by his fear and pragmatism, felt himself unable to try. In fact, he was determined to do just the opposite.

Horrified by the prospect of revolution and dismayed by the defeat of his party and its principles, Harper retired from politics in 1801. In a widely reprinted farewell letter to his constituents, he lauded Federalist accomplishments and forewarned voters that if Republicans "by their rashness their feebleness or their folly, destroy the fair fabric of national happiness which their predecessors have erected; should they embroil the nation unnecessarily with its neighbours, or suffer to fall into ruin those domestic establishments which have bestowed on it such unexampled

---

24. Mary Brown to Tomes Birtum, 11 March 1790, Black Children's Papers, 1790-1802, Friends Historical Library of Swarthmore College.

prosperity; the day of account and retribution will soon come, and a dreadful day it will be." Harper seems to have reacted to the "revolution of 1800" in much the same way that his family adjusted to his own rebellion: first with tenacious opposition and then reluctant resignation. In ballot after ballot he supported Aaron Burr until, faced with no alternative, he cast a blank vote.[25]

Fearful for the nation's future, Harper resettled in Maryland, a "middle ground" where slavery's presence was less pronounced.[26] There was at that time a "scarcity of eminent Lawyers" in Baltimore, and through his renowned defenses of Judge John Pickering and Justice Samuel Chase, Harper quickly established one of the city's leading law practices. According to a young Republican observer, "Harper, although inferior to Luther Martin, and perhaps several others, as a mere lawyer, was, notwithstanding, generally considered as the head of the profession".[27]

---

25. The same year as Jefferson's election, Gabriel's aborted slave rebellion confirmed Harper's deepest misgivings about the dangers of French influence on American slaves. See Douglas R. Egerton, *Gabriel's Rebellion: The Virginia Slave Conspiracies of 1800 and 1802* (Chapel Hill: University of North Carolina Press, 1993), 46, 115; RGH, *A Letter from Robert Goodloe Harper, of South Carolina, to His Constituents* (Portsmouth, N.H.: Charles Peirce, 1801), reprinted in Cunningham, 1: 247-65; and RGH to Burr, 24 December 1800, in Mary Jo Kline, ed., *Political Correspondence and Public Papers of Aaron Burr*, 2 vols. (Princeton: Princeton University Press, 1983), 1: 474-75.

26. Barbara Jeanne Fields, *Slavery and Freedom in the Middle Ground: Maryland During the Nineteenth Century* (New Haven: Yale University Press, 1985); Elaine G. Breslaw, ed., "'Freedom Fettered': Blacks and the Constitutional Era in Maryland, 1776-1810," *Maryland Historical Magazine* 84 (Winter 1989): 297-369.

27. RGH to Hampton, 26 September 1799, filed with the miscellaneous documents for *Hampton v. Harper*, Judgments, Court of Appeals, MSA; Lynn W. Turner, "The Impeachment of John Pickering," *American Historical Review* 54 (April 1949): 485-507; *Annals of Congress*, 8th Congress, 1st Session, 328-43; James Haw, Francis F. Beirne, Rosamond R. Beirne, and R. Samuel Jett, *Stormy Patriot: The Life of Samuel Chase* (Baltimore: Maryland Historical Society, 1980); Hoffer and Hull, 206-55; Paul S. Clarkson and Jett, *Luther Martin of Maryland* (Baltimore: Johns Hopkins Press, 1970); and Henry Marie Brackenridge, *Recollections of Persons and Places in the West* (Philadelphia: James Kay, 1834), 164-65. Upon moving to Maryland, Harper's partisan quarrels with the soon-to-be Governor, John Francis Mercer, almost led to their dueling. While Harper and his Federalist colleagues Chase and Martin turned away from their moderate antislavery opinions and grew increasingly conservative in the 1790s, Mercer stayed true to his populist Antifederalist ideals. See Eric Robert Papenfuse, "Unleashing the 'Wildness': The Mobilization of Grassroots Antifederalism in Maryland," *Journal of the Early Republic* 16 (Spring 1996): 73-106.

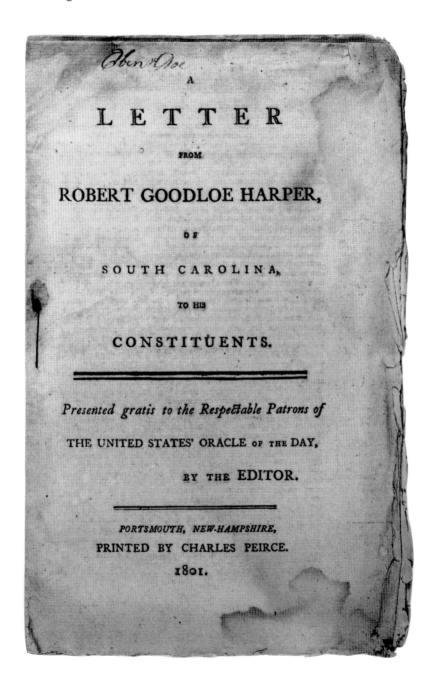

FIGURE THREE. Harper's farewell address. Original in the collections of the author. Photograph courtesy of the Maryland State Archives.

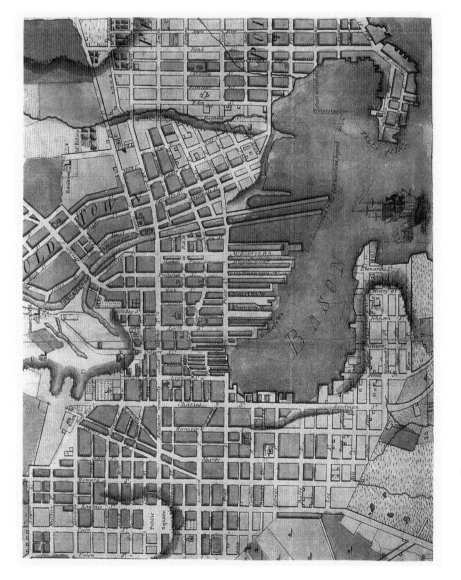

FIGURE FOUR. Baltimore at the turn of the century. Detail from [Charles Varle], *Warner and Hanna's Plan of the City and Environs of Baltimore*, 1801. Original in the Peabody Library Collection of the Johns Hopkins University. Photograph courtesy of the Maryland State Archives.

In the admiralty court he was unrivalled; there his political information and general knowledge had a field for display, while his mind was not cramped by that technicality and dry precision which was necessary in the courts of common law. He was by no means a thorough bred, acute, discriminating lawyer....He was an elegant debater; a finished scholar, with a mind stored with various reading, and perfect command of language; but his manner was not of that earnest, vehement kind, which is most popular at the bar. His deportment and manners were those of a dignified gentleman, his bust and features extremely fine, and if I may so express it, *á l'antique*.

In May 1801 Harper, "a well formed man, of middle stature, and uncommonly full chest; and then much in fashion in his personal appearance," married Catherine Carroll, daughter of Charles Carroll of Carrollton.[28] Their unhappy union provides a metaphor for Harper's relationship with slavery. Chronically depressed, Catherine constantly complained to her husband. In one noticeably emotional dispatch, she lamented:[29]

There is a passage in your letter that gives me great pain, as I cannot Misunderstand it....[Although] you are not happy, at home, & with me, you have the consolation that many men have not, of being removed from the Object that causes that unhappiness, at least 9 months out of 12—Those three months, my Husband, you must bear with patience & fortitude, a little while longer. Heaven will at last hear your prayer & remove the Cause of your misery.

Never a particularly loving husband, Harper spent extended periods of

28. The description of Harper is by his friend William Sullivan in *Familiar Letters of Public Characters...* (Boston: Russell, Odiorne, and Metcalf, 1834), 107. Harper was married by Bishop John Carroll, and as a result, he must have at least tacitly converted to Catholicism.

29. Catherine often referred to herself as poor, sick, and neglected. See Catherine Harper to RGH, Friday Night & Monday Night [1805], HPP, MHSL. For Harper's understanding of gender relations, see Thomas Lowndes to RGH, 27 March 1787, Thomas Lowndes Papers, SCL; RGH to Morris, 15 July 1792, Morris Papers, New-York Historical Society (NYHS), New York City; RGH to Sullivan, 17 March 1797, William Sullivan Papers, Library of Congress (LC), Washington, D.C.; and generally Stephanie McCurry, *Masters of Small Worlds: Yeoman Households, Gender Relations, & the Political Culture of the Antebellum South Carolina Low Country* (New York: Oxford University Press, 1995).

time away from his Gay Street mansion in order to escape his wife. Yet, while he could neglect her in favor of business in Washington and Annapolis, she, like slavery, remained ever pressing on his mind. Just as the peculiar institution was the economic foundation of the country, Catherine was the source of Harper's wealth. Over the course of their marriage, Charles Carroll of Carrollton gave the couple more than $86,958 in cash. His resources restored Harper's credit and permitted the lawyer to pursue many speculative enterprises. Though Harper tried selfishly to do so, he could not in the end avoid recognizing that he was both reliant on and responsible for his wife. Their bond, like the country's marriage to slavery, was "for better or for worse."[30]

After the passage of the Embargo, Maryland Federalism experienced a slight resurgence, and Harper returned to politics. In 1810 he became president of the Washington Society of Maryland, a group designed "to support, extend and carry into effect the political principles and system of [George] Washington."[31] This organization was part of a larger

---

30. This cash figure does not include property and other assets given to the Harpers. Carroll kept meticulous records of his finances, and thus the totals are relatively easy to establish. See Cox, 212-14; Edward C. Papenfuse, Jr., "Charles Carroll of Carrollton: English Aristocrat in an American Setting," in *"Anywhere So Long as There Be Freedom": Charles Carroll of Carrollton, His Family & His Maryland* (Baltimore: Baltimore Museum of Art, 1975), 42-57; and the bond signed by Carroll and Harper to Hampton for $25,000, *Hampton v. Harper* documents, MSA. In 1802 Harper was so indebted to his father-in-law and apprehensive of a slave rebellion that he likely played a key role in manufacturing evidence to prevent a large number of Carroll's slaves from winning their freedom in *Mahoney v. Ashton.* For a detailed analysis of this important legal battle, see Eric Robert Papenfuse, "From Recompense to Revolution." Since this article's publication, new material has come to light which suggests that the liberty of "upwards of fifteen Hundred" slaves throughout Maryland was in fact at stake. See Philip E. Thomas to John Parrish, 1 January 1804 & 24 December 1805, Cox-Parrish-Warton Collection, HSP; Joshua Civin, "The Cost of Joining: The Maryland Abolition Society, Its Successors, and the Meaning of Voluntary Association, 1789–1819" (Senior Essay, Yale University, 1996).

31. Alexander Contee Hanson described the society's members in a letter to Harper soon after the organization was founded. "In the short span of three days," wrote Hanson, "one hundred and thirty odd members have been enlisted among which are the most respectable young & old men of all professions including several influential mechanics. The list is heavily increasing & promises to be long in members & respectability." In 1806, hoping to win popular support for his stalled congressional campaign, Harper had drafted the charter for Baltimore's Mechanics Bank. During these years, though he read avidly, spent long hours compiling his *Select Works*, and fully dedicated himself to becoming a respected "Philosopher," he still found the time to serve as a director of the Baltimore Water Company, a manager of the Baltimore Dancing Association, and as a

(continued...)

movement by Federalist leaders to establish "benevolent" institutions throughout the country. Most modern historiographic interpretations of the societies differ only slightly from the critiques by contemporary Republicans.[32]   According to one report published in August 1811, Maryland's Washington Society was run by an unscrupulous group of Federalists who hoped to swindle "wealthy blockheads" by inducing them to make "large donations, a great proportion of which, instead of being dedicated to benevolence," were "used for no other purpose than the printing and distribution of handbills and pamphlets."[33]

Yet for Harper the Washington Society was much more than a partisan vehicle for disseminating Federalist propaganda; it was a

---

31.(...continued)

member of both the Baltimore Library Company and the Delphian Club. See Hanson to RGH, 3 March 1810, Robert Goodloe Harper Papers (RGHP), LC; RGH to Harrison Gray Otis, 27 May 1806, Harrison Gray Otis Papers, MHS; *The Constitution of the Washington Society of Maryland* (Baltimore: John L. Cook, 1810); RGH, *Select Works...*, vol. 1 (Baltimore: O. H. Neilson, 1814); Victor Sapio, "Maryland's Federalist Revival, 1808-1812," *Maryland Historical Magazine* 64 (Spring 1969), 1-17; L. Marx Renzulli, Jr., *Maryland: The Federalist Years* (Rutherford, N.J.: Fairleigh Dickinson University Press, 1972); Frank A. Cassell, "The Structure of Baltimore's Politics in the Age of Jefferson, 1795-1812," in Aubrey C. Land et al., eds., *Law, Society, and Politics in Early Maryland* (Baltimore: Johns Hopkins University Press, 1977), 277-96; Charles G. Steffen, *The Mechanics of Baltimore: Workers and Politics in the Age of Revolution, 1763-1812* (Urbana: University of Illinois Press, 1984); Bailey, 263; and Eric Robert Papenfuse, "'The Dead Shall Speak for Us': The Washington Society of Maryland, 1810-1813," unpublished manuscript.

32. The foremost historian of the societies is Fischer. He argues that they were a means through which Federalists "acclimatized" themselves to the world in which they lived. Other scholars have been less charitable in their assessments. James M. Banner, Jr., contends that the organizations were "ostensibly" magnanimous, but "in reality" they were little more than partisan vehicles for disseminating "Federalist propaganda." Paul A. Varg goes so far as to claim that the groups "had little relationship to the first president and even less to benevolence." Steven Watts dismisses their importance altogether. In his judgment the associations' efforts inaccurately reflect the "spirit of the age" since younger Federalists were motivated by "a cynical desire for elite manipulation rather than popular involvement." See Shaw Livermore, Jr., *The Twilight of Federalism: The Dis-integration of the Federalist Party, 1815-1830* (Princeton: Princeton University Press, 1962), 12–13; Fischer, *The Revolution of American Conservatism: The Federalist Party in the Era of Jeffersonian Democracy,* (New York: Harper & Row,1965), 110-28; Banner, *To the Hartford Convention: The Federalists and the Origins of Party Politics in Massachusetts, 1789-1815* (New York: Alfred A. Knopf, 1970), 264; Varg, *New England and Foreign Relations, 1789-1850* (Hanover, N. H.: University Press of New England, 1983), 68; and Watts, *The Republic Reborn: War and the Making of Liberal America, 1790-1820* (Baltimore: Johns Hopkins University Press, 1987), xxii, 13.

33. *Maryland Republican,* 5 August 1811; Baltimore *Whig,* 7 August 1811.

"laudable, useful, and necessary" platform from which he could address the issues that plagued his conscience. As Linda Kerber has suggested, venerating Washington allowed Federalists to accept "the American Revolution while at the same time rejecting the French Revolution as chaotic." Washington's greatest accomplishment, proclaimed one member of the Maryland Society, was that he had "prevented the revolution [against Great Britain] from falling into anarchy" at the very moment when it "threatened to degenerate into a mere treasonable rebellion."[34]

In speeches by Harper and other Federalist leaders, Washington became an amalgamation of Jesus and Moses. Not only was he a this–worldly deliverer who had led his country from English Bondage to the Promised Land of Independence, but he was also an otherworldly redeemer whose continual resurrection offered hope of eternal salvation. As Harper explained, "His mission to this world was not confined to the benefit, which while living he might bestow on this country. It was part of his sublime vocation to live for us beyond the grave; and to leave us in his example a guide for our conduct, through all future eyes."[35] Ironically, this spiritual homogenization of Jesus and Moses was also common among slaves. Like Harper, black men and women struggled to maintain hope in a world in which revolution was unacceptable. "Jesus, once become Moses," asserts Eugene Genovese, "...solved the problem of how to achieve spiritual freedom, retain faith in earthly deliverance, instill a spirit of pride and love in each other, and make peace with a political reality within which revolutionary solutions no longer had much

34. RGH to Hanson, 5 March 1810, RGHP, LC; Kerber, *Federalists in Dissent: Imagery and Ideology in Jeffersonian America* (Ithaca: Cornell University Press, 1970), 5-10; and Charles Wallace Hanson, *Oration Delivered Before the Washington Society of Maryland, on the Twenty-Second February, 1811* (Baltimore: John L. Cook, 1811), 14.

35. The Exodus theme is best expounded in Charles Hanson's speech. "We see him," wrote Hanson, "encountering all the perils and terrors of a desert...pursuing with an undaunted unprecedented perseverance the deliverance of his countrymen." See Hanson, *Oration*, 5; RGH, *An Oration, on the Birth of Washington; Delivered Before the Washington Society of Alexandria, by Robert Goodloe Harper, One of Its Members, on the 22d. of February, A.D. 1810...* (Alexandria: S. Snowden, 1810), 14; and Robert P. Hay, "George Washington: American Moses," *American Quarterly* 21 (Winter 1969): 780-91. According to Upton Heath, Washington, like Moses, had to make every effort "to subdue the spirit of rebellion, and to silence the murmurs of discontent....He stood in the midst of these dangers, as a lofty mountain around whose summit, in vain the tempests beat, and the lightenings gleam terrific." See Heath, *Oration Delivered Before the Washington Society of Maryland, on the Twenty-Second February, 1812* (Baltimore: Magauran and Kennedy, 1812), 12-16.

prospect."[36]

For Society members, Washington's *Farewell Address* became a new covenant. Each received his own copy, and an officer read the document aloud before meetings. "Adhere to the principles of Washington...and ye shall live," declared Harper. Fail to obey his commandments, and "the day of retribution" would arrive.[37] Harper warned of how a "monster, the most fierce and sanguinary and relentless that has hitherto ravaged the earth, with his fangs fixed in the almost lifeless carcase of continental Europe, now casts his eye, with a baleful and malignant scowl, on our happy country." Unless the nation abided by Washington's doctrine of neutrality, Americans would be forced:[38]

> to see their sons torn from their studies, their occupations, or from the arms of a youthful bride and the caresses of a tender infant, and driven to perish by disease or the sword in distant climes; to be expelled from their houses, or forced to receive guests who convert them into menial servants: to see their wives exposed to outrage, and their daughters the prey of violence or seduction; [these] are some of the horrors which march in the train of foreign domination.

As a freshman Congressman from South Carolina, Harper had witnessed Washington's magical allure. In 1796 he wryly observed, "No man however popular, had the least chance of becoming an elector if he was understood to be opposed to the old man." Yet now the nation's first President had come to embody all the traits that Harper most admired. Steadfast in his ways and willing to suffer public persecution rather than compromise his beliefs, Washington "was never known to be diverted or driven from his purposes, by any anticipated loss of popular favor." "Prudent and cautious," he "only drew his sword from necessity," and he never provoked a fight "when unable to meet the enemy in battle."

---

36. Genovese, *Roll, Jordan, Roll: The World the Slaves Made* (New York: Pantheon, 1974), 254-55. Blacks in New York founded the "Washington Benevolent Society of Africa." See Dixon Ryan Fox, "The Washington Benevolent Society," *Columbia University Quarterly* 21 (January 1919), 31.

37. *Washington's Farewell Address* (Baltimore: John L. Cook, 1810); Baltimore *Federal Republican*, 24 February 1812; RGH, *Oration Delivered Before the Washington Society of Maryland, on the Fourth of July, 1810* (Baltimore: John L. Cook, 1810), 12; and William Magruder, *An Oration on the 5th of July, at the New Theatre, Before the Washington Society of Maryland, and Published at their Request* (Baltimore: Sergeant Hall, 1813), 12.

38. RGH, Alexandria *Oration*, 14; RGH, Baltimore *Oration*, 10.

Indeed, Washington "continually found new resources in the midst of disaster and universal dismay." Harper and other Federalists felt that they must do likewise if the social order were to be sustained.[39]

Just as the first President's resurrected spirit soothed Harper's fears, the charitable activities of the Washington Society renewed his faith in the transformative power of education. Article IX of the society's constitution specified that a Washington Free School was to be established in order to provide for the training of "as great a number as possible of poor children." To accomplish this end, the society adopted the Lancasterian system of teaching.[40] Similar schools had been established in New York, Philadelphia, and throughout Europe. Directed primarily at the lower classes of society, these institutions provided efficient, economical education for the masses.[41] By 1812, as Alexander

---

39. RGH to Alexander Hamilton, 4 November 1796, quoted in Barry Schwartz, *George Washington: The Making of an American Symbol* (New York: Free Press, 1987), 77; RGH, Alexandria *Oration*, 5–6; and Heath, *Oration*, 9, 20. See also Michael T. Gilmore, "Eulogy as Symbolic Biography: The Iconography of Revolutionary Leadership, 1776-1826," in Daniel Aaron, ed., *Studies in Biography* (Cambridge: Harvard University Press, 1973), 131-57; Lawrence J. Friedman, *Inventors of the Promised Land* (New York: Alfred A. Knopf, 1975), 48; James H. Smylie, "The President as Republican Prophet and King: Clerical Reflections on the Death of Washington," *Journal of Church and State* 18 (Spring 1976): 233-52; and Simon P. Newman, "Principles or Men? George Washington and the Political Culture of National Leadership, 1776–1801," *Journal of the Early Republic* 12 (Winter 1992): 477-507.

40. Very little is known about the specific workings of the Washington Free School. Alexander Contee Hanson wrote to Harper complaining that the school was "very much in need of Lancaster's tools, cards, among others." The Lancasterian method encouraged learning through fierce competition between students. Often, tickets, which were redeemable for prizes such as books, balls, and toys, were awarded to pupils who demonstrated high levels of achievement. The "cards" which Hanson mentioned probably refer to the large lesson boards from which a single monitor would teach a group of students. See A. C. Hanson to RGH, 23 February 1812, HPP, MHSL; Carl F. Kaestle, *Joseph Lancaster and the Monitorial School Movement* (New York: Teachers College Press, 1973), 1-54.

41. John Franklin Reigart, *The Lancasterian System of Instruction in the Schools of New York City* (New York: Columbia University, 1916); William R. Johnson, "'Chanting Choristers': Simultaneous Recitation in Baltimore's Nineteenth-Century Primary Schools," *History of Education Quarterly* 34 (Spring 1994): 1-23. Lancaster eventually settled in Baltimore, where he established the Lancasterian Institute. See Lancaster, *The Lancasterian System of Education with Improvements* (Baltimore: Wm. Ogden Niles, 1821), xv. Harper made several contributions. See RGH to Joseph Lancaster, 13 December 1823, 23 January 1824, & 27 March 1824, Joseph Lancaster Papers, Manuscript Division, American Antiquarian Society; Lancaster to RGH, 12 December 1823 & 24 January 1824, Misc. Mss. L, NYHS.

FIGURE FIVE. The Lancasterian method. Reprinted from Joseph Lancaster, *The British System of Education*, 1810. Original in the Yale University Libraries. Photograph courtesy of the Maryland State Archives.

Contee Hanson described in a letter to Harper, the Washington Free School had begun to fulfill the sanguine expectations of its founders:[42]

> We paraded nearly an hundred boys belonging to the school, which consists of 109 and is constantly increasing. You would have been delighted to hear their examinations. Two of them delivered orations which astonished the company....The effect of their handsome appearance on the stage was very much heightened by the handsome appearance of the boys and their teacher.

Anticipating the spread of wisdom and knowledge throughout the land, Harper looked with hope toward the future. In his mind, the Washington Free School was a factory, churning out converts of the "true religion." Mass baptism, it seemed, would redeem the nation. In the meantime, by stressing respect and obedience, his school would help preserve the fragile social structure. Within Lancasterian schools, harmony was maintained in a strict, military fashion. Each student was permitted to maximize his innate potential, but all learned their proper place in society's grand "machine." Students who misbehaved were punished severely. Some were forced to wear "shackles" on their feet and elbows or "logs" around their necks. Others were yoked together in a "caravan" and forced to walk backwards. Perhaps the most dreadful of all punishments was "the basket." Disobedient boys who earned this discipline were "put in a sack" and "suspended to the roof of the school, in sight of all the pupils, who frequently smile[d] at the birds in cage." Lancaster believed that corporal punishment was essential, and when criticized by horrified spectators, he defiantly responded:[43]

---

42. A. C. Hanson to RGH, 23 February 1812, HPP, MHSL. Three weeks after war was declared against Great Britain, the Exeter *Constitutionalist* applauded the generous "liberality and philanthropy" of Maryland's Washington Society. A rival New Hampshire newspaper countered that the "principal object" of these Federalists had since degenerated. Still, both papers agreed that Baltimore's school had, at least for a short while, profoundly influenced society. See Exeter, *Constitutionalist and Weekly Magazine*, 7 July 1812; Concord *New-Hampshire Patriot*, 2 March 1813.

43. Sterling Fishman, "The Double-Vision of Education in the Nineteenth-Century: The Romantic and the Grotesque," in Barbara Finkelstein, ed., *Regulated Children Liberated Children: Education in a Psychohistorical Perspective* (New York: Psycho—history Press, 1979), 111—12; Finkelstein, "Reading, Writing, and the Acquisition of Identity in the United States: 1790-1860," in ibid., 119-123; and Lancaster, *The British System of Education: Being A Complete Epitome of the Improvements and Inventions Practised at the Royal Free*
(continued...)

> The reader must know, that there are in this *wicked world* many
> *Knights of the Rod*, who wish to perpetuate the reign of ignorance
> among the lower classes of society, whom they are pleased to consider
> "DOOMED *to the drudgery of daily labour*," and that "*learning to
> write and cypher*" will render them "*discontented with their lot.*"...One
> of these *hired* advocates of ignorance, in a silly phrensy, imagined,
> that the apparatus of logs, shackles, caravans, &c. were all implements
> of slavery....Neither he, nor the other *conspirators* against the
> education of youth, considered the more degrading severity of the
> lash, which these punishments have for years, contributed to
> annihilate.

Like Harper, Lancaster believed that "ignorance" was the greatest evil
threatening the domestic security of a free nation. Both men readily
acknowledged that, in certain environments, individual rights and personal liberties had to be forfeited in order to maintain a well–regulated
and "enlightened" society.

If the goals of Maryland's Washington Society were to be taken
literally, Harper's school could easily have included blacks. "In selecting
the objects of this charity," read the organization's charter, "the prefer-
ence shall always be given to the members of the society, whose situation
may render them unable to provide for the suitable education of their
children."[44] At that time in Baltimore, there were several schools for
African–Americans.[45] It is unlikely, however, that the Washington Free
School included people of color; Harper would have found such an
undertaking too dangerous.[46] Nonetheless, by allowing him to implement his educational philosophy without having to confront directly the
moral dilemma of slavery, "poor children" became psychological

---

43.(...continued)
Schools, Borough-Road, Southwark (London: Longman and Co., 1810), 34-38.

44. The same had been true for the Cambridge literary society more than twenty years
earlier.

45. In 1811, for example, a Methodist Episcopal church purchased property on Sharp
Street in order to expand its school for black children. The property cost $1,000. See
James M. Wright, "The Free Negro in Maryland, 1634-1820," *Studies in History, Economics
and Public Law* (New York: Columbia University, 1921), 202-204.

46. In 1811, several blacks were training at Lancaster's Borough Road Institution in
England in order to bring his educational system to Sierra Leone. See Mora Dickson,
Teacher Extraordinary: Joseph Lancaster, 1778-1838 (Sussex, England: Book Guild Limited,
1986), 127.

equivalents for those whom he was unable and unwilling to assist. The school's accomplishments restored Harper's faith in America's improvement and humanity's progress by assuring him that the long and arduous process of "teaching, learning, [and] obeying the law" had begun and that an earthly Promised Land might one day be reached.

Then, in the summer of 1812, the Baltimore riots forced the Washington Free School to disband.[47] The previous winter, Federalist members of the Washington Society had begun carrying weapons in order to protect themselves from angry Republicans. Tensions reached a fevered pitch four days after war was declared against England, when a mob destroyed Alexander Contee Hanson's Baltimore office of the *Federal Republican* in a protest against its anti–war editorials. When Hanson returned to Baltimore and attempted to distribute his paper from a fortified brick building, a second mob attacked. Two men were killed, and many others were badly beaten.[48] Such violence devastated Harper. Baltimore had become the "Paris of America," and no longer could he ignore the fears that festered inside him. In public, Harper supported Hanson and disparaged the mob's actions, but in private, he lamented, "The liberty of the press might, I think, have been defended, and better defended, without coming to Baltimore."[49]

Demoralized by the closing of the Washington Free School, and extremely "apprehensive"of the "violent convulsion" that war with England seemed destined to produce, Harper grew increasingly despon-

---

47. Listings for the Washington Free School can be found in the *Baltimore City Directory* for 1812; *Mnemonika: or, Chronological Tablets....* (Baltimore: B. W. Sower for Edward J. Coale, 1812), 337. The school was located at the corner of Lemmon and East Streets in downtown Baltimore. On the decline of the Washington Benevolent Societies, see generally Lawrence D. Cress, "'Cool and Serious Reflection': Federalist Attitudes toward War in 1812," *Journal of the Early Republic* 7 (Summer 1987): 123-45.

48. In many respects what happened in Baltimore was the racial inversion of Harper's greatest fear. Poor whites rose up, attacked slaves, and destroyed the property of free blacks. See Cassell, "The Great Baltimore Riot of 1812," *Maryland Historical Magazine* 70 (Fall 1975): 241-259; Hickey, "The Darker Side of Democracy: The Baltimore Riots of 1812," *Maryland Historian* 7 (Fall 1976): 1-19; Paul A. Gilje, "The Baltimore Riots of 1812 and the Breakdown of the Anglo–American Mob Tradition," *Journal of Social History* 13 (Summer 1980): 547-64; and idem, "'Le Menu Peuple,' in America: Identifying the Mob in the Baltimore Riots of 1812," *Maryland Historical Magazine* 81 (Spring 1986): 50-66.

49. Hickey, *The War of 1812: A Forgotten Conflict* (Urbana: University of Illinois Press, 1989), 68; RGH to A. C. Hanson, 26 August 1812, HPP, MHSL. Symbolically, the rioters smashed the presses of the *Federal Republican*, the medium through which the Federalists were trying to "educate" Baltimoreans.

dent.[50] It was many months before a "providential" turn in world affairs would restore his spirit. This time, Harper drew inspiration not from the legacy of Washington but from the triumphant acts of Alexander I of Russia, for whom he felt a great affinity. Like Harper, Alexander was a champion of public education who had reached the conclusion that human bondage was an evil necessity.[51] During the Tsar's reign, several universities, forty-two secondary schools, and over two-hundred Lancasterian schools were established throughout Russia.[52] As Alexander defeated the French and broke the "fetters" and "chains" that constrained Europe, he simultaneously "delivered" Harper.[53] Not only did he remove "the iron yoke" under which Europe "writhes and bleeds and groans," but, according to Harper, he also saved the "civilized world" from "the pit prepared for its destruction":[54]

---

50. RGH to Benjamin Stoddert, 10 September 1812, HPP, MHSL; Roger H. Brown, *The Republic in Peril: 1812* (New York: Columbia University Press, 1964).

51. One of Alexander's biographers has written, "If Americans, with their traditions of freedom and egalitarianism, still fail to live up to their professed ideals with respect to a mere tenth of their fellow citizens more than a century after emancipation—for which a civil war had been required—maybe allowance can be made for Alexander's backing and filling when faced with the reconstruction of Russian society....His liberal ideals were sincere but subject to his fears of the unknown." See Allen McConnell, *Tsar Alexander I: Paternalistic Reformer* (Arlington Heights, Illinois: Harlan Davidson, 1970), 204-208; Peter Kolchin, *Unfree Labor: American Slavery and Russian Serfdom* (Cambridge: Harvard University Press, 1987), 143-47.

52. Nicholas V. Riasanovsky, *A History of Russia: Fourth Edition* (New York: Oxford University Press, 1984), 302-307; Kaestle, 32.

53. Harper called Alexander "THE DELIVERER." It is important to note that British antislavery forces considered Alexander to be a central factor in abolishing the international slave trade. One year after Harper's oration, William Wilberforce and several others met with the young Tsar in London, and they were apparently quite impressed with his commitment to antislavery principles. See extracts from William Allen's memorandum book, 19 June 1814, cited in Betty Fladeland, *Men and Brothers: Anglo-American Antislavery Cooperation* (Chicago: University of Illinois Press, 1972), 101; John Pollock, *Wilberforce* (London: Constable, 1977), 239-47.

54. RGH, *Address of Mr. Harper at the Celebration of the Russian Victories, In Georgetown, District of Columbia; on the 5th of June, 1813* (Georgetown: James B. Carter, 1813), 16, 36-37. Daniel Webster commented to a friend that he believed Harper's speech was "very good." See Webster to Charles March, 6 June 1813, NYHS; John Carroll to Enoch Fenwick, 8 June 1813, in Thomas O'Brien Hanley, ed., *The John Carroll Papers*, 3 vols. (Notre Dame: University of Notre Dame Press, 1976), 3: 225-26. For Harper's military service in the War of 1812, see William M. Marine, *The British Invasion of Maryland, 1812–1815* (Baltimore: Society for the War of 1812 in Maryland, 1913), 160-69, 313.

The Conspiracy against Baltimore, or the War Dance at Montgomery Court House

FIGURE SIX. *The Conspiracy against Baltimore, or the War Dance at Montgomery Court House*, circa 1812. Original in the Maryland Historical Society. Photograph courtesy of the Maryland State Archives. Harper, seated, is conniving with the Devil-figure, Hanson, while other bloodthirsty Federalists dance and scheme nearby.

Those hands from which his powerful arm has stricken off the shackles, are every where lifted up to invoke blessings on his name. Hope dawns again on the nations.—Those whom the light has not yet reached, behold it afar off, and bless its approach.—Those who, like us, had not yet been overwhelmed, but stood looking with awful and trembling anxiety on the impending storm, now see it dispelled, and begin again to act freely.

In speeches before the Washington Society, Harper had constructed a European allegory for the problem of slavery. Unable to face his own world, he had projected his anxieties onto the imperial contests abroad. Napoleon was the "master"; the peasants of Europe were his "slaves." If Americans looked across the Atlantic, Harper wrote:

They will see the labourer worn out with toil, reposing on a bundle of straw, or on the cold bare ground, often having divided with his half-naked wife & children, the scanty & miserable meal, which forms their only repast. They will see his wretched hut, the abode of filth & vermin, without a candle to light it or a fire to dispel the damp, where himself, his family and his few domestic animals, if he should be so fortunate as to have any, are crowded together on a space hardly sufficient to give each room for extending his length on the floor; while the fruits of his labour are rung from him, by a thousand oppressive devices, leaving him and his family just on the brink of starving, to support those pageants which are so much admired.

Such had been the case before Napoleon's defeat; now, thanks to Alexander, this misery would not spread to America. "The emancipation of Europe is secured," rejoiced Harper in January 1814. "We are saved from the chains prepared for us."[55] At last able to "act freely," Harper no longer withheld his support for the war against Britain. In September he fought bravely at the Battle of North Point and two months later was commissioned a major-general.

First by devoting his energies to the educational enterprises of the

---

55. RGH, Baltimore *Oration*, 4-8; RGH, Alexandria *Oration*, 3-8, 14; RGH, *Speech of Robert Goodloe Harper, Esq., at the Celebration of the Recent Triumphs of the Cause of Mankind in Germany. Delivered at Annapolis, Maryland, January 20, 1814* (New Haven: Oliver Steele, 1814), 3; and William Gribbin, *The Churches Militant: The War of 1812 and American Religion* (New Haven: Yale University Press, 1973), 52.

Maryland Washington Society and later by focusing his attention on the contest for freedom in Europe, Harper had deflected his thoughts from the moral dilemma of slavery in America. With the restoration of peace and the demise of his party, he would find it increasingly difficult to put aside his fears of a domestic slave rebellion. Ignoring the peculiar institution and projecting his anxieties elsewhere had not made the evils of this system disappear. Over the last decade of his life, Harper would grow ever more convinced that slavery's presence had to be physically, not psychologically, removed before it was too late.

CHAPTER THREE

Colonization and Diffusion: The Only Solutions

WHEN ROBERT GOODLOE HARPER learned of the Hartford
Convention in the fall of 1814, he unequivocally condemned its
proceedings. In his mind secession was a dangerous strategy that would
ultimately prove ineffective. Since the germs of factionalism had now
spread throughout the "entire nation, "the "root" of the "evil" could no
longer be "cut out to effect a cure." Rather, the political schemes of New
England Federalists, much like the inflammatory rhetoric of Quakers,
would only exacerbate the country's ills. Harper drew a similar analogy
when discussing slavery. The "natural body," he argued, personified the
"body politic." Slavery was a "cancer," slowly eating "its way to the vitals
of the state," and localized remedies could not forestall its corrosive
effects:[1]

> [A]s, no part of the human body can be Infected without impairing the
> health comfort & strength of the whole; as a gangrene cannot exist in
> the hand or the foot, any more than in the head or the breast, without
> endangering the life of the patient; so a cause of weakness disease or
> decay cannot exist in any Section of the country or any portion of the
> community without affecting the political health & endangering the
> safety of the nation at large.

For Harper, diffusion and colonization thus seemed "the only means" of
ameliorating "the alarming evil of the black population." Either "the
inflammation...which, if confined to one spot, or one limb, might be
sufficient to produce gangrene, or the most painful and dangerous ulcers,"
could be "dispersed through the whole system" so that it proved "too
inconsiderable to be felt"; or the affliction could slowly be purged from
the body of the nation. Unless such remedies were adopted, the country
would surely perish.[2]

---

1. RGH to Sullivan, 2 November 1814, HPP, MHSL; RGH, "Committee Report," 5
March 1824, in *The Seventh Annual Report of the American Society for the Colonization of
Free People of Colour of the United States* (Washington: Davis and Force, 1824), 113; RGH,
"Speech before the American Colonization Society, February 20, 1824," in ibid., 7
(Colonization Speech); and Noah Worcester to RGH, 3 December 1824, BPL.

2. RGH, "To the Voters of the Congressional District of the City and County of
(continued...)

As we have seen, slavery embodied two great evils that threatened
Harper's world and racked his conscience. First, it was a moral sin,
perpetually degrading blacks, stifling their ability to learn, and condemning them to an unthinking life without "true religion." Second, it was a
political evil, engendering "a certain class of men" prone to revolution.
Consequently, the United States was "pregnant with future danger."
Convinced that slavery's "dark cloud" could no longer be ignored, Harper
embraced colonization and diffusion as alternatives to the status quo. "If
a hostile army threatened to invade a portion of these United States," he
reasoned, "would it not afford a legitimate employment for the army and
the fleet?" If so, surely "[we] are not bound to wait till the moment when
they are to be used. This would be as unsafe, I might even say as futile, as
to delay making the fortifications of the Country, till the moment of
invasion or attack."[3]

In many respects, the South's system of labor, to extend Harper's
anthropomorphic comparison, had sent the whole nation into "labor."[4]
The pain of childbirth could be viewed as just punishment for the
"original sin" of slavery; America's salvation, like Harper's own, rested
upon the ability to atone for past wrongs. Just as a natural period of gesta-
tion existed before a baby could leave his mother's womb, emancipation
had to occur gradually—though Harper reasoned it would take not nine
months but "two centuries." In the meantime, he insisted, slavery had to
be tolerated. Indeed, the stakes were too high to dally with unrealistic talk
of abolition. Such plans, by offending the "strong feelings" and opinions
of "nearly half the Union," threatened to abort the possibility of a permanent solution for slavery. Alarming the Southern "sensibility," "which,
whether well founded or not, is extremely keen," was unwise, for it
promised "to excite and to foster" the "far greater and more certain evil"

---

2. (...continued)
Baltimore," 1824, HPP, MHSL (Baltimore Speech); RGH, "General Harper's Speech in
the Senate of Maryland, January 19, 1820, On the Resolution from the House of
Delegates, Relative to the Missouri Question," *Federal Gazette and Baltimore Daily
Advertiser*, 7-10 February 1820, reprinted as Appendix C below (Missouri Speech).

3. RGH, Colonization Speech, 7-8; RGH, Baltimore Speech.

4. The historian Lawrence Friedman has offered an intriguing comparison between
colonization and "the human defecation process." For Harper, however, childbirth seems
a more accurate metaphor. See Friedman, "Purifying the White Man's Country: The
American Colonization Society Reconsidered, 1816-1840," *Societas* 6 (Winter 1976), 1-24.
Friedman goes too far when he concludes that for the prototypical colonizationist "the
rhetoric, not the reality, was what really mattered." See idem, *Inventors of the Promised
Land*, 213-14.

FIGURE SEVEN. Robert Goodloe Harper. Marble bust by Raimondo Trentanove, 1819. Original in the Maryland Historical Society. Photograph courtesy of the Baltimore Museum of Art.

of domestic "divisions by geographical lines."[5]

In 1817, after serving briefly in Washington as a senator from Maryland, Harper actively began championing the cause of African colonization.[6] "It tends," he wrote in his first public defense of the movement, "and may powerfully tend, to rid us gradually and entirely in the United States, of slaves and slavery: a great moral and political evil, of increasing virulence and extent, from which much mischief is now felt, and very great calamity in future is justly apprehended."[7] The idea of colonization was not new.[8] In *Notes on the State of Virginia*, first published in 1785, Thomas Jefferson wrote that blacks ought to be "colonized to such a place as the circumstances of the time should render most proper, sending them out with arms, implements of household and of the handicraft arts, seeds, pairs of the useful domestic animals &c. to declare them a free and independent people...." Like Harper, Jefferson considered slavery a "great political and moral evil." As long as the institution existed, "a revolution of the wheel of fortune" was imminent in which slaves and their masters would exchange places. Although Jefferson believed that blacks could not be assimilated into society due to their natural inferiority and the permanent "stain" of their color, something nevertheless had to be done to eradicate slavery's ill effects. Accordingly, he embraced a policy that sought to relocate blacks rather than integrate them within the community.[9]

The first extensive movement for the colonization of American blacks in Africa began in 1816. The historian Douglas Egerton has argued that Charles Fenton Mercer, not the Reverend Robert Finley, was re-

---

5. RGH, Missouri Speech.

6. Harper was elected in 1816 but resigned at the end of the year in order to return to his legal practice. See Fischer, "Robert Goodloe Harper," 160-64.

7. RGH, *A Letter from Gen. Harper, of Maryland, to Elias B. Caldwell, Esq. Secretary of the American Society for Colonizing the Free People of Colour, in the United States, with their own Consent* (Baltimore: R. J. Matchett for E. J. Cole, 1818), 11, reprinted below as Appendix B.

8. See Peter Kent Opper, "The Mind of the White Participant in the African Colonization Movement, 1816-1840" (Ph.D. Dissertation, University of North Carolina, 1972), 1-26.

9. Jefferson, *Notes on the State of Virginia*, 138; John Chester Miller, *The Wolf by the Ears: Thomas Jefferson and Slavery* (New York: Macmillan, 1977), 45; P. J. Staudenraus, *The African Colonization Movement, 1816-1865* (New York: Columbia University Press, 1961), 1. That men as diverse in their thinking as Jefferson and Harper could unite behind a single cause demonstrates the movement's broad base of support as well as the widespread optimism surrounding its initial conception.

sponsible for its organization.[10] Harper knew both men and had already backed Samuel J. Mills in his efforts to educate and resettle free blacks in the northwestern United States. When Harper learned of Mercer and Finley's newly formed American Colonization Society, he quickly became devoted to their program.[11] In fact, it was he who gave Liberia its name. As John H. B. Latrobe would later recall, "Various names were suggested, and Freedonia was on the point of being adopted; when General Harper said, 'Can nothing be made of Liber, a free man?'" When Harper died in 1825, Latrobe, memorializing his mentor's long years of loyal service, bemoaned the society's "irreparable loss" and lamented that "its right arm" had been "severed from its body in Maryland."[12]

Harper's most important tract on colonization was a widely circulated 1817 letter to the Society's Secretary, Elias Caldwell, detailing the chief reasons for supporting this "great enterprise." American slavery,

---

10. Even if Mercer provided the motivating stimulus for colonization, historians should not necessarily follow Egerton's advice and reevaluate "the society, its goals, and its failures." A "religiously inspired, benevolent, [and] mildly emancipationist" interpretation should not be replaced by "a class-oriented" one. Both types of supporters were extremely important. See Egerton, "'Its Origin is not a Little Curious': A New Look at the American Colonization Society," *Journal of the Early Republic* 5 (Winter 1985), 463-80; idem, *Charles Fenton Mercer and the Trial of National Conservatism* (Jackson: University Press of Mississippi, 1989). Still useful are Henry Noble Sherwood, "The Formation of the American Colonization Society," *Journal of Negro History* 2 (July 1917): 209-28; Early Lee Fox, *The American Colonization Society, 1817–1840* (Baltimore: Johns Hopkins Press, 1919).

11. Harper joined both the American Colonization Society and its auxiliary in Maryland. He eventually became a vice president of the latter but was only able to give $30, the lowest sum of any lifetime member. As a point of comparison, his father-in-law gave $100. See *The Third Annual Report of the American Society for Colonizing the Free People of Colour of the United States* (Washington: Davis and Force, 1820), 133; C. W. Sommerville, *Robert Goodloe Harper* (Washington: Neale Company, 1899). Before joining the colonization movement, Harper was a member of the Protection Society of Maryland, an association dedicated to "establishing a society for ensuring protection to the people of color who are now free, and to those who, at a future period, will be entitled to their freedom." See the Society's 1816 Constitution in *Maryland Historical Magazine* 1 (1906): 358-62. For discussions of this group's intentions as well as its organized efforts to prevent the kidnapping and wrongful imprisonment of free blacks, see Civin; *Federal Republican*, 9 October 1816. On Mills, consult Staudenraus, 18-19; Marks, 7; and Gardiner Spring, *Memoirs of the Reverend Samuel J. Mills.* (New York: J. Seymour, 1820).

12. Latrobe studied law with Harper and later became president of the American Colonization Society. See Latrobe, *Colonization and Abolition* (Baltimore: John D. Toy, 1852), 9; John E. Semmes, *John H. B. Latrobe and His Times, 1803-1891* (Baltimore: Norman, Remington, 1917), 142. The town of Harper in Liberia is named after RGH, who also gave the name Monrovia to the colony's capital. See generally Penelope Campbell, *Maryland in Africa: The Maryland State Colonization Society, 1831–1857* (Urbana: University of Illinois Press, 1971).

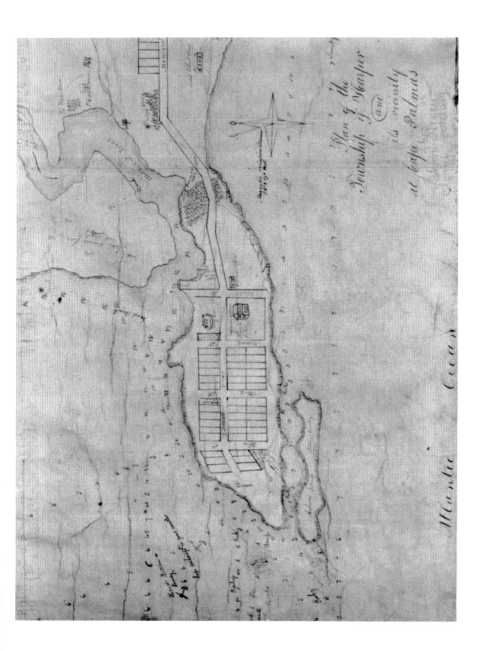

FIGURE EIGHT. A map of Harper, Liberia, circa 1840. Courtesy of the Maryland Historical Society.

Harper explained, was unique to history because of its racial foundation. In every other country slaves were and always had been of the "same race, origin, colour and general character" as their masters. Accordingly, upon manumission the former slave could easily partake "in all the benefits of freedom." In the United States, however, "You may manumit the slave, but you cannot make him a white man." Because of the "indelible mark" of their color, blacks were "condemned to a state of hopeless inferiority and degradation." White racial "prejudices" created an "impassible barrier," which blacks could never hope to overcome:[13]

> Be their industry ever so great and their conduct ever so correct, whatever property they may acquire, or whatever respect we may feel for their characters, we never could consent, and they never could hope, to see the two races placed on a footing of perfect equality with each other: to see the free blacks or their descendants visit in our houses, form part of our circle of acquaintance, marry into our families, or participate in public honours and employments. This is strictly true of every part of our country, even those parts where slavery has long ceased to exist, and is held in abhorrence. There is no state in the union, where a negro or mulatto can ever hope to be a member of congress, a judge, a militia officer, or even a justice of the peace: to sit down at the same table with the respectable whites, or to mix freely in their society.

Harper used the example of Paul Cuffe to support his argument. Cuffe, part African and part Native American, was a prosperous merchant and an enthusiastic promoter of colonization. "Respectable, intelligent and wealthy," he was, to Harper, the epitome of what blacks could become under the proper conditions. Yet even Cuffe harbored "no expectation or chance of ever being invited to dine with any gentleman in Boston, of marrying his daughter, whatever may be her fortune or education, to one of their sons, or of seeing his son obtain a wife among their daughters." Ostracized by the color of his skin, Cuffe was prevented from coexisting on an equal social level with whites, despite his intellectual achievements and high moral standing. If Cuffe, a well–known and widely respected half–Indian who actively supported the American Colonization Society, could never become fully assimilated within white America, in Harper's estimation, no black ever would.[14]

---

13. RGH, *A Letter*, 5-8.

14. RGH, *A Letter*, 7. It is important to note Harper does not argue that Cuffe's progeny should be prevented from marrying the children of white Bostonians. Rather, he asserts

(continued...)

Many of Harper's assertions concerning the strength of prevailing racial prejudices are supported by Cuffe's own recollections. In April 1812, when returning from an expedition to Sierra Leone, Cuffe's ship and cargo were confiscated by American authorities for illegally transporting British goods. Having no other recourse, Cuffe traveled to Washington where he petitioned James Madison for the release of his property. The amiable President not only restored Cuffe's ship but applauded his efforts at colonization. Nonetheless, as he triumphantly departed the Capitol, Cuffe met "a blustering powder headed man with stern countenance" who forced him to give up his carriage seat. In addition, when he finally arrived in Baltimore, they "utterly refused" to take him in at the tavern or serve him dinner unless he went "back among the servants." These incidents, recorded in Cuffe's personal journal, vividly illustrate the powerful racism at work in Harper's home city. Cuffe was a rich, well-educated, partially black man, but even on the day when the President of the United States praised his intentions and returned his ship, he could not ride or dine where he pleased.[15]

It is one thing to be told that you are inferior, and quite another to internalize that debasement. Clearly, a man like Cuffe did not believe himself of lesser ability than whites. Yet, for Harper, Cuffe was the exception. Without hope of advancement, the "vast majority" of free blacks lost all "desire" to improve their condition and became "an idle, worthless and thievish race." Though these men and women were not born this way, Harper insisted, they were "rendered so by their own degradation":[16]

14.(...continued)
that they had "no expectation or chance" of ever doing so. Perhaps, since he could not envision racial intermixture, this is a slight and subtle difference. Yet, it does seem that Harper feared miscegenation to much less of an extent than many of his contemporaries. See Jordan, 542-69.

15. Lamont D. Thomas, *Rise to Be a People: A Biography of Paul Cuffe* (Chicago: University of Illinois Press, 1986); Sherwood, "Paul Cuffe," *Journal of Negro History* 8 (April 1923): 153-232; and Sheldon H. Harris, *Paul Cuffe: Black America and the African Return* (New York: Simon and Schuster, 1972).

16. RGH, *A Letter*, 8-10. For more than half a century, historians have denounced the "proslavery" and "racist" motivations of Harper and other colonizationsists. Strongly negative appraisals of the movement can be found in William Lloyd Garrison, *Thoughts on African Colonization* (Boston: Garrison and Knapp, 1832); Charles I. Foster, "The Colonization of Free Negroes, in Liberia, 1816–1835," *Journal of Negro History* 38 (January 1953): 41-66; Philip C. Wander, "Salvation Through Separation: The Image of the Negro in the American Colonization Society," *Quarterly Journal of Speech* 57 (February 1971), 57-67; Stephen L. Cox, "'Polluted With the Blood of Africa': Bigotry, Slavery, and the New Hampshire Colonization Society," *Historical New Hampshire* 38
(continued...)

The debasement which was at first compulsory, has now become habitual and voluntary. The incitement to good conduct and exertion, which arises from the hope of raising himself or his family in the world, is a stranger to his breast. He looks forward to no distinction, aims at no excellence, and makes no effort beyond the supply of his daily wants; and the restraints of character being lost to him, he seeks, regardless of the future, to obtain that supply, by the means which cause him the least present trouble.

Harper thought that free blacks posed an even greater danger to white society than did slaves. In many respects they remained "equals" except for the former's "exemption from the authority of a master." Both groups were condemned to a life of temporal bondage, and neither had any prospect of self–improvement. Yet unlike their strictly–disciplined brothers, free blacks seemed violent and malicious, setting "traps and snares for the young and thoughtless slaves." Without a master to oversee them and keep them ignorant, free blacks grew wiser. Having been exposed to basic precepts of learning, they quite foreseeably became dissatisfied with the helplessness of their condition and soon degenerated into wickedness and debauchery.[17] One of Harper's deepest fears was that this example would agitate the dormant slave population:[18]

16.(...continued)
(Summer/Fall 1983): 117-40; Larry E. Tise, *Proslavery: A History of the Defense of Slavery in America, 1701–1840* (Athens: University of Georgia Press, 1987), 50-54, 230-32; and George M. Fredrickson, "Comment," *Intellectual History Newsletter* 14 (1992): 17-20. The problem with such approaches is that they fail to reflect the wide–ranging, complex, and often contradictory goals of colonization's leading proponents. Nor do they take into account the changing natures of the American Colonization Society and its auxillaries over the course of the antebellum period. More helpful in this regard are David M. Streifford, "The American Colonization Society: An Application of Republican Ideology to Early Antebellum Reform," *Journal of Southern History* 45 (May 1979): 201-20; William W. Freehling, "'Absurd' Issues and the Causes of the Civil War: Colonization as a Test Case," in *The Reintegration of American History: Slavery and the Civil War* (New York: Oxford University Press, 1994), 138-57; and, most significantly, Davis, "Reconsidering the Colonization Movement: Leonard Bacon and the Problem of Evil," *Intellectual History Newsletter* 14 (1992): 3-16.

17. RGH, A Letter, 10-11.

18. Harper's fear of free blacks was probably influenced by their noticeable growth in his home city. From 1810-1820, the free black population of Baltimore nearly doubled from 5,671 to 10,326. See Fields, 62; RGH, *A Letter*, 9-11; and Arthur Zilversmit, *The First Emancipation: The Abolition of Slavery in the North* (Chicago: University of Chicago Press, 1967), 222-29. For recent scholarship that contradicts Harper's negative caricature of free blacks and gives evidence of the many, varied contributions of Baltimore's thriving African–American community, see Leroy Graham, *Baltimore: The Nineteenth Century*
(continued...)

The slave seeing his free companion live in idleness, or subsist, however scantily or precariously, by occasional desultory employment, is apt to grow discontented with his own condition, and to regard as tyranny and injustice the authority which compels him to labour. Hence he is strongly incited to elude this authority, by neglecting his work as much as possible, to withdraw himself from it altogether by flight, and sometimes to attempt direct resistance.

Ironically, blacks imperiled the peace and prosperity of Harper's world not because they were inferior brutes but because they were rational human beings. It was the capacity to learn that made both slaves and free blacks so threatening:

The alarming danger of cherishing in our bosom a distinct nation, which can never become incorporated with us, while it rapidly increases in numbers, and improves in intelligence; learning from us the arts of peace and war, the secret of its own strength, and the talent of combining and directing its force: a nation which must ever be hostile to us, from feeling and interest, because it can never incorporate with us, nor participate in the advantages which we enjoy: the danger of such a nation in our bosom need not be pointed out, to any reflecting mind.

Once placed within a "proper situation" where they would not have to compete against overwhelming racial prejudice, Harper believed that blacks would become "a virtuous and happy people." Until that time, however, they would be unable to enjoy the "freedom, civilization, and christianity" that was their birthright. Thus, Harper's support for colonization rested in part upon the assumption that slaves would be able to overcome their disabilities in a new environment:[19]

---

18. (...continued)
Black Capital (Washington: University Press of America, 1982); C. W. Phillips, "Negroes and Other Slaves: The African–American Community of Baltimore, 1790–1860" (Ph.D. Dissertation, University of Georgia, 1992); and T. Stephen Whitman, "Slavery, Manumission, and Free Black Workers in Early National Baltimore," (Ph.D. Dissertation, Johns Hopkins University, 1993). For the Early Republic more generally, see Ira Berlin, *Slaves without Masters: The Free Negro in the Antebellum South* (New York: Pantheon, 1974); Shane White, *Somewhat More Independent: The End of Slavery in New York City, 1770–1810* (Athens: University of Georgia Press, 1990); Nash and Jean R. Soderland, *Freedom By Degrees: Emancipation in Pennsylvania and Its Aftermath* (New York: Oxford University Press, 1991); and Donald R. Wright, *African Americans in the Early Republic, 1789–1831* (Arlington Heights, Illinois: Harlan Davidson, 1993).

19. RGH, *A Letter*, 11-12, 17-18.

Here they are condemned to a state of hopeless inferiority, and consequent degradation. As they cannot emerge from this state, they lose by degrees the hope and at last the desire of emerging. With this hope and desire they lose the most powerful incitements to industry, frugality, good conduct, and honourable exertion. For want of this incitement, this noble and ennobling emulation, they sink for the most part into a state of sloth wretchedness and profligacy. The few honourable exceptions serve merely to show of what the race is capable, in a proper situation. Transplanted to a colony composed of themselves alone, they would enjoy real equality: in other words real freedom. They would become proprietors of land, master mechanics, ship owners, navigators and merchants, and by degrees schoolmasters, justices of the peace, militia officers, ministers of religion, judges, and legislators. There would be no white population to remind them of, and to perpetuate, their original inferiority; but enjoying all the privileges of freedom, they would soon enjoy all its advantages, and all its dignity.

In Harper's mind this scenario appeared entirely plausible when contemplating the history of European colonization and the future of western migration.[20] As he exhorted the citizens of Baltimore, "[Look West.] Reflect on its recent settlement, its rapid growth, and its present magnitude. Not long since a trackless wilderness, an almost impenetrable forest, roamed over by wild beasts, hunters and savage tribes." If these lands could be developed, so too could Africa become a "great nation." Harper's faith in the transformative power of technology fueled his optimism. "It is no light matter," he wrote, "to make a canal ninety-two miles long, over a most rugged country, and across four rivers requiring aqueducts; one of which must be upwards of a mile in length, and two others a quarter of a mile each." Yet it could be done. For one willing to spend millions of dollars on canals, roads, and other domestic improvements, the expense of colonization hardly seemed prohibitive.[21]

Quite simply, for Harper, African colonization was not a far-fetched

---

20. Opper makes this point by quoting Harper's son, Charles, who wrote to Ralph Gurley in 1829 comparing the Liberian settlers to "the early Pilgrims to our country." See Opper, 37.

21. In 1827 Henry Clay estimated that colonization would cost only one million dollars a year. See Davis, "Reconsidering the Colonization Movement," 13; RGH, *General Harper's Speech on Canals* (Baltimore: Edward J. Coale, 1824), 11, 22; John Lauritz Larson, "'Bind the Republic Together': The National Union and the Struggle for a System of Internal Improvements," *Journal of American History* 74 (September 1987): 363-87; and idem, "Jefferson's Union and the Problem of Internal Improvements," in Onuf, ed., *Jeffersonian Legacies* (Charlottesville: University Press of Virginia, 1993), 340-69.

or half–hearted dream.[22]   The critical factor was establishing a viable colony, and by 1824, with Liberia a reality, everything seemed in place:

> A colony is actually established, in a healthy situation; peace has been secured; the means of supply and of sustenance are provided; all is done that needs to be done to complete the experiment, and to prove the practicability of the plan proposed.

At last, "the blessings of knowledge and freedom" would spread to a "continent that now contains 150 millions of people, plunged in all the degradations of idolatry, superstition, and ignorance."[23]   Harper genuinely believed that most Southern planters would assist in emigration by embracing a plan of compensated manumission.   It was in their best interests, he argued, since free labor was far more efficient and prosperous than slavery.[24]   While white workers strove to "produce as much and consume as little as possible," slaves did just the opposite:

> What the slave consumes is for himself: what he produces is for his master. All the time that he can withdraw from labour is gained to himself; all that he spends in labour is devoted to his master. All that the free labourer, on the contrary, can produce is for himself. All that he can save is so much added to his own stock. All the time that he loses from labour is his own loss.

Slavery also proved detrimental to the work ethic among poor whites:[25]

---

22. As Davis has written, "Although the colonizationists have conventionally been dismissed as hopelessly impractical visionaries, for example, they were clearly more realistic than the abolitionists when they argued that white racial prejudice would remain intractable for generations to come, that the achievements of a few individual blacks would not benefit the masses, that progress would depend on black solidarity and collective effort, and that the formal act of emancipating slaves could not be divorced from the need for an economic and social environment in which freedmen could exercise their full capacities for human development." See Davis, "Reconsidering the Colonization Movement," 3.

23. Harper was obsessed with geography and even equipped a mulatto named Abel Hurd to scout the area for him. Hurd died in Africa. See Semmes, 140; RGH, *A Letter*, 23-32; RGH, "Colonization Speech," 7-9; and generally Amos Jones Beyan, *The American Colonization Society and the Creation of the Liberian State: A Historical Perspective, 1822–1900* (Lanham, Md.: University Press of America, 1991).

24. Modern scholarship has shown this to be an erroneous perception. See Robert W. Fogel, *Without Consent or Contract: The Rise and Fall of American Slavery* (New York: W. W. Norton, 1989).

25. RGH, *A Letter*, 13-14; Fredrickson, *The Black Image in the White Mind: The Debate on*
(continued...)

They who continually from their infancy see black slaves employed in labour, and forming by much the most numerous class of labourers, insensibly associate the ideas of labour and of slavery, and are almost irresistibly led to consider labour as a badge of slavery, and consequently as a degradation. To be idle, on the contrary, is in their view the mark and the privilege of freemen.

Still, one major stumbling block stood in Harper's way. Free blacks were largely unwilling to leave. Indeed, it is not surprising that free blacks were among the first to attack the colonizationists' motives. In January 1817, for example, 3,000 black Philadelphians overwhelming rejected colonization at a meeting in Bethel Church even though several highly respected black ministers advocated the enterprise. Despite the professed desire of Harper and his colleagues to extend a "paternal arm" to Africa, they were clearly using blacks to advance "the interests of the United States."[26] For his part, Harper had always assumed that blacks would want to go to Liberia. Since they were rational creatures, he was confident they would eventually realize that colonization offered their only hope for improvement. Black opposition, he theorized, would be short-lived:

> These people it is said, especially the industrious and estimable part of them, will not go to the new colony. That many of them will decline to go at first, and some always, cannot be doubted. It is even probable, and may safely be admitted, that but few of them now think favourably of the project: for men, especially ignorant men, venture unwillingly upon great changes, the extent nature and consequences of which they are little capable of understanding. But it by no means follows that the same unwillingness or hesitation will continue, after the ground shall have been broken, the way opened, and a settlement formed.

Soon Harper felt himself forced to conclude that many blacks simply were not "intelligent" enough to discern "the advantages of the undertaking." More education would be necessary before they would forsake their unwarranted apprehensions and perceive the numerous benefits of re-

---

25.(...continued)
Afro–American Character and Destiny, 1817–1914 (New York: Harper & Row, 1971), 1-42.

26. Nash, *Forging Freedom: The Formation of Philadelphia's Black Community, 1720–1840* (Cambridge: Harvard University Press, 1988), 237-39; RGH, "Colonization Speech," 7, 16. See also Louis R. Mehlinger, "The Attitude of the Free Negro toward African Colonization," *Journal of Negro History* 1 (June 1916): 276-301; Marie Tyler McGraw, "Richmond Free Blacks and African Colonization, 1816–1832," *Journal of American Studies* 21 (August 1987): 207-24.

FIGURE NINE. *Thoughts of Liberia: Emancipation.* Oil on canvas by Edwin White, 1861. Courtesy of the New-York Historical Society.

turning to Africa.[27] Yet before Harper was able to address this dilemma, the Missouri Controversy erupted, and once again, domestic turmoil threatened to destroy his world. Hurrying to Annapolis, Harper took William Winder's seat in the state legislature, and on February 7, 1820, he rose to speak. There, before the senate, stood a peculiar man "of middle height, straight as an arrow, strongly rather than delicately built, square shouldered, of a florid complexion and very bald, with regular features, an aquiline nose, clear gray eyes, and compressed lips, of formal carriage and precise speech."[28] Undoubtably, Harper felt this was the most important oration of his life. His precariously balanced universe was teetering, and it would take all his eloquence to restore some semblance of order. In a long and carefully reasoned plea, he advocated diffusion of the slave population, a suggestion that modern historians have often ridiculed.[29] For Harper, however, the idea was neither proslavery in sentiment nor disingenuous.[30] In his judgment slavery's extension through space was a necessary prerequisite for its gradual extinction through time. Not only was this scheme made necessary by the current state of society, but it was directly in keeping with the moral philosophy he had espoused through-out his life:[31]

> [I]t will I think be admitted by all, who have the slightest knowledge of the subject, that in proportion as the slaves are dispersed, in proportion as they are less accumulated in masses and in particular districts, their moral condition and qualities are improved; and the political and moral evils to be apprehended from slavery are diminished. If, for

---

27. RGH, *A Letter*, 21; Opper, 33.

28. The exact circumstances of Harper's return to politics are somewhat clouded. See Fischer, "Robert Goodloe Harper," 169-71. The description of Harper is Latrobe's. See Semmes, 109-10. Latrobe continued, "...my dear old master at the end of half a century stands now before my mental vision as if I had parted from him within the hour. I see him in his blue coat and buff waistcoat, his tight pantaloons, and highly polished and carefully fitted boots, with his feet turned out in soldierly fashion, laying down the law to me in the office as to the jury in the Court room with a clearness and accuracy of expression such as few men possessed. Always cool, never excited, speaking always in the same agreeable voice, he was a model of a forensic orator....As a writer of pure English, he had no superior in the profession."

29. See, for example, Don E. Fehrenbacher, *The South and Three Sectional Crises* (Baton Rouge: Louisiana State University Press, 1980), 8-23.

30. For modern interpretations of the diffusionists similar to my own, see Freehling, *The Road To Disunion: Secessionists at Bay, 1776-1854* (New York: Oxford University Press, 1990), 151; Drew R. McCoy, *The Last of the Fathers: James Madison and the Republican Legacy* (Cambridge: Cambridge University Press, 1989), 265.

31. RGH, Missouri Speech.

instance, five individuals possess two hundred slaves each, on five adjoining plantations, these thousand slaves will certainly be very inferior, in a moral point of view, to the same number dispersed among five hundred farmers, each of whom has two; or some four or five and some none at all. They may not be more abundantly fed, more warmly clad, or better situated for the mere multiplication of the species; but they will enjoy more individual freedom, more actual liberty, more association with their masters and the families and equals of their masters, and more means of instruction, intellectual, moral, and religious: they will be governed with more ease, and consequently with less rigour, will occupy in short a higher rank in the scale of being, and become more respectable moral agents.

Diffusion, to Harper, was a legitimate means of redeeming blacks and eradicating slavery, not spreading its evils. By allowing blacks to become "more respectable moral agents," it offered them the ability to transcend their temporal degradation and prepare for the life to come. Without the dispersal of slavery's "dark cloud," otherwise benevolent masters would be forced to withhold the "true religion" from their slaves. Many masters, contended Harper, wanted to treat their slaves more humanely but simply could not, given the high concentration of slaves and the ever-present threat of revolt. "It can I think hardly be doubted," he wrote, "that there would be more danger from a thousand slaves, collected together in a small district, than from the same number dispersed over two or three counties, among a much more numerous free white population." By diffusing this danger, moral and social progress would occur.[32]

In his speech before the Maryland legislature, Harper argued that, although the federal government had the Constitutional authority to restrict the spread of slavery, it would be "inexpedient" to do so in this instance.[33] Missouri's poor climate and the high costs of transportation led to a general "unsuitability of the country for the profitable employment of slaves." Thus, regardless of federal legislation, it could not "long continue a slaveholding state." Malthusian restrictionists, who believed that the slave population would increase as more food supplies became available, were likewise mistaken. Slavery would stay "the same in its

32. James Madison also believed that "restriction would most likely unleash instead a devastating cycle of repression, resistance, and violence, thereby inflaming rather than diffusing the dilemma of slavery." See McCoy, 273; RGH, Missouri Speech.

33. Harper was one of only a few prominent Southerners who contended that the national government had the constitutional authority to prohibit the western expansion of slavery. See Glover Moore, *The Missouri Controversy, 1819-1821* (Lexington: University of Kentucky Press, 1953), 226; Robert Pierce Forbes, "Slavery and the Meaning of America, 1819–1833" (Ph.D. Dissertation, Yale University, 1994).

aggregate amount," insisted Harper, whether or not it was extended into the territories:

> [I]f you leave all these emigrants at home, the population of the parent country will increase no faster and no more, than if you take them away; because this population being regulated by the ordinary means of subsistence, or, more properly speaking, by the facility of obtaining subsistence, cannot rise above a certain point, and will attain that point.

The North had little to worry about, in any case, because the South was a dying power. Since slavery was inherently wasteful and retarded population growth, its economy would never be able to keep pace with Northern industry. Hence, it was unwise to start a war when all that was required was patience.[34]

Harper's unabashed proclivity to wait "for many ages to come," along with his self-proclaimed "dispassionate view" of slavery, reveal a man unwilling and perhaps unable to acknowledge the daily atrocities of human bondage. While he sympathized with the plight of America's slaves only on a highly theoretical and detached plane, he maintained a steadfast conviction in the natural equality of all races. In fact, he blamed white prejudice for many of the ills of contemporary society, sincerely believed that colonization and diffusion would lead to the eventual abolition of slavery, and was ultimately realistic in his prediction that a civil war alone could bring about the slow and difficult process of full-scale black integration into American society. Harper continued to expound many of the same principles in the last years of his life that he had so vigorously advocated more than thirty-five years earlier in the back hills of South Carolina.[35] As he wrote in 1824 in a speech that he did not live long enough to present, he planned to devote the remainder of his days to the "internal improvements & the Colonization of the blacks with their own consent, & the consent of those who may have a right to their service." Most importantly, he hoped that eventually the national government would be able to "provide for the purchase & education of any number, or all, of the children of colour who now are or hereafter shall be born, provided their owners will agree to sell them, and for their transportation at a suitable age to Liberia, & other similar settlements,

---

34. RGH, Missouri Speech.

35. See, however, [RGH] *Plain Reasons of a Plain Man, For Preferring Gen. Jackson to Mr. Adams, As President of the United States* (Baltimore: Benjamin Edes, 1825).

hereafter to be formed, on the Southwestern Coast of Africa."[36]

In a contemplative letter that Harper wrote two months before his death, he confided to the Reverend Leonard Bacon that he had long had such ideas "at heart." Now, more than ever, the United States had to turn its "attention wholly to the rising generation" of blacks, all of whom desperately needed to be embraced "in a great scheme of education." No longer could white Americans block the path to blacks' redemption and their own, by withholding teaching and instruction. The benefits of "knowledge and the true religion," urged Harper, must be permitted to enlighten the impressionable hearts and minds of such youth, whether slave or free. His dream was the founding of "a seminary farm" for such children in Maryland that might serve as a model for similar institutions throughout the nation.[37] Harper envisioned that one hundred students between the ages of ten and fourteen would be sent to the school "with the consent of their parents when free and their owners when slaves." Convinced that many slaveholders earnestly desired to emancipate their slaves but lacked an acceptable means of doing so, he anticipated that numerous "contributions in young slaves" would undoubtably be made "as soon as the establishment" were "ready for their reception."

At the seminary farm, blacks would be able to acquire "all the necessary improvements" that would prepare them for life in Liberia. Boys would be instructed in the proper methods of agriculture and "all the common handicraft trades, such as smiths, shoemakers, carpenters, and others." Girls would "be kept in separate apartments, and employed under suitable female instructors, in all the departments of domestic industry, household occupations, household manufactures, and the various employments suitable for females of the laboring class." Both sexes would be "taught reading, writing and the rudiments of arithmetic," and "all the young persons" would "be required to attend religious worship, and to receive religious instruction." Furthermore, those found to "possess particular aptitudes" at certain tasks would be permitted to maximize such potential.

Harper predicted that after an initial deficit the school would become economically viable. All proceeds from the sale of crafts and produce would be appropriated by the "Establishment" and used to defray the school's expenses. The students would be credited for their labor at fixed

---

36. RGH, Baltimore Speech.

37. Harper hoped that Bacon would fund the school. RGH to Bacon, 8 November 1824, Bacon Family Papers, Manuscripts and Archives, Yale University, reprinted below as Appendix D. Bacon's views on colonization were quite similar to Harper's. See Davis, "Reconsidering the Colonization Movement."

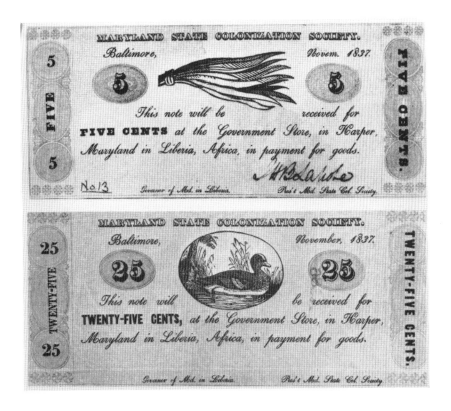

FIGURE TEN. Liberian currency.   Original in the Maryland Historical Society. Photograph courtesy of the Maryland State Archives.

rates but charged rent, board, and a superintendence fee. Any resulting surplus would then be "invested in a savings bank to accumulate for the benefit of the child and to form a fund for its outfit on its removal, at a proper age to the colony." Thus, Harper's plan was a means of both equipping blacks to go to Liberia and simultaneously defraying the costs of their transportation.

The seminary farm was hardly a utopian commune. While in attendance, all children would be enslaved, including those who were free and wished to participate. Apparently, Harper had concluded that not only was slavery tolerable in some circumstances, but sometimes had to be induced if its evils were ever to be mitigated. Discipline at the school was to be kept with strict military precision, and, as Harper emphasized:

> [T]he most effectual means will be adopted and enforced, for preventing all...open communication between these young people themselves, or with others beyond the pale of the seminary. To render these means effectual, is one great object of locating the seminary in a state where slavery exists, and where alone the proper authority, for this and other purposes, can be exercised.

Just as the institution of slavery would be undermined if exposed to the spirit of learning, blacks could not be educated without being restrained by the discipline of slavery. For Harper, slavery and freedom had proven an inescapable paradox.

In January 1825 Robert Goodloe Harper suffered a sudden fatal heart attack. Unable to find a sponsor for his school, he had continued to hope that one day all of the country's blacks would be "drawn from their degraded situations, fitted for an higher condition and transported without shock or convulsion" to their new homeland across the Atlantic. These dreams, however, proved elusive. His extravagant lifestyle and failed land speculations left his family so mired in debt that at his death his own twenty-seven slaves remained in bondage.[38]

---

38. Baltimore County Register of Wills (Inventories), WK 1071-1072, pp. 225-32, MSA. Upon learning of Harper's death, one ardent New England abolitionist wrote to her relation in Boston, "The death of the good Gen. Harper at such a time, is particularly lamentable. Was his benevolent plan respecting the African school, ever gone into operation?" See Mary Clark to Francis Jackson, 28 July 1825, Francis Jackson Papers, MHS.

AFTERWORD

A View from the Grave

THOUGH ROBERT GOODLOE HARPER was nearly sixty years old when he died, news of his sudden passing came as a shock to many. For nearly a month after his death, members of the Baltimore bar and officers in the state's First Brigade donned black mourning bands to honor their respected general's memory. By all accounts Harper's funeral was a grand affair. Scores of dignitaries and well-wishers attended the service and gazed solemnly as a procession of distinguished Marylanders carried the dead man's casket to the family's private burial ground at Oakland. William Wirt, the United States Attorney General, observed in a letter to his daughter:[1]

> I have just returned from General Harper's funeral. This letter will probably bring you the first account of his death. He dropped down dead, on Friday morning, (the 14th,) and, it is said by his physicians, died probably before he reached the floor. He has had no recent warning of the probable approach of death. On the contrary, he has been unusually well for some time past. On Thursday, he was well in court, and made one of the best arguments he ever made in his life—an argument three hours long. I met him again, in the afternoon, at a watch-maker's, and he told me that he did not experience the slightest inconvenience from his exertions in speaking in the morning, and that he never felt better. That night he was at a ball, and, I am told, was uncommonly gay and agreeable. On Friday morning he was again well, had eaten his breakfast as usual, and was standing up before the fire, reading a newspaper, when death struck him in the manner I have mentioned. No one was in the room but his son, a fine young man of nineteen, and a little negro boy.

One can only imagine what the room looked like that fateful morning when Harper finished his breakfast, picked up a newspaper, and walked slowly towards the fire. Oakland's original farmhouse was

---

1. John P. Kennedy, *Memoirs of the Life of William Wirt*, 2 vols. (Philadelphia: Blanchard and Lea, 1852), 2: 169; Baltimore *American Farmer*, 18 January 1825.

demolished in the 1920s, and no photographs of the estate are known to have survived. The Harpers' extravagant tastes are well documented. In 1803 after subsidizing still another of the couple's purchases, Charles Carroll of Carrollton begged his son-in-law to moderate his lavish expenses and "cease ordering any more... furniture." In all likelihood the room where Harper died was adorned with imported fabrics, elegantly crafted chairs, and intricate plaster moldings. What would "the little negro boy" have thought as his master stood before him "uncommonly erect" amidst this opulent display of wealth and finery? Perhaps, as Harper's lifeless body collapsed onto the floor, the child was dreaming of a new home in Liberia. More likely, he was reflecting on the day's chores. Certainly the servant had no idea that in March 1825, when an inventory would be made of his deceased owner's estate, all the "chattel" then living at Oakland would be appraised at too high a value to be granted their freedom.[2]

Yet rather than attempt to piece together the scene at the moment of Harper's death, let us move ahead in time to the year 1848. Of Harper's six children, only his daughter Emily is still living. Charles Carroll Harper, the "fine young man" mentioned in Wirt's letter, died more than a decade earlier at the youthful age of thirty-five. His wife and eleven-year-old daughter have been forced to sell portions of the estate but still reside at Oakland, in an 1830s mansion built according to General Harper's specifications and filled with relics from the family's illustrious past. Hanging prominently on the dining room wall can be seen a portrait of Robert Goodloe Harper in his Revolutionary War uniform. Diagonally across from it, perched high on a pedestal, is a marble bust of the first President, carved by the Italian sculptor Raimondo Trentanove. Immediately to the left, above the mantle of the fireplace, rests a framed engraving of Jonathan Trumbull's *Declaration of Independence*, one of the family's most cherished items, for before he died in 1835 Charles Carroll of Carrollton had been the document's last surviving signer.

It is five minutes to one. Mrs. Harper and her daughter have just finished their midday meal. Their guest this afternoon is a longtime friend

---

2. "Oakland," Vertical File, Enoch Pratt Free Library, Baltimore; Carroll of Carrollton to RGH, 7 January 1803, HPP, MHSL; J. S. Watson to unknown, 17 February 1804, in "Letters from William and Mary College," *Virginia Magazine of History and Biography* 29 (April 1921), 170; Trentanove to RGH, 16 August 1821, Robert Goodloe Harper Papers, Duke University Library; and Baltimore County Register of Wills (Administrative Accounts), 1825-1827, book 24, p. 329, MSA.

of the family who has recently returned from the Mexican War. Seated round the table, both women listen eagerly to the wounded veteran's tales of adventure. No one notices when the servants, hoping to learn the latest news, enter the room and begin to clear the dishes. At last the story reaches its climax and the soldier, gesturing at the portrait on the wall, proudly proclaims that the general would surely have approved of these glorious exploits, the first-fruits of America's manifest destiny. As he makes his point, the visitor turns toward the fire only to behold two ghostly images: a tired old man staring dejectedly at the floor, and another man in his mid-forties who appears slightly saddened by what he has just heard. The male servant, once a "little negro boy" and now a full-grown man, instantly recognizes the aged figure slumped in the chair by the fire as his former master, with his son Charles Carroll Harper standing at his side.

This ethereal encounter is not entirely the product of my imagination. Richard Caton Woodville, a young Baltimore artist, painted a strikingly similar scene in 1849 while studying in Dusseldorf, Germany. Among Woodville's companions was William Pennington, a fellow Marylander who would eventually marry Charles Carroll Harper's daughter, the young lady in the center of the painting. Robert Goodloe Harper's close friend and law student, John H. B. Latrobe, was one of Woodville's principal American benefactors at this time. Woodville painted his 1848 masterpiece, *Politics in an Oyster House*, for Latrobe, and as Harper's devotee, Latrobe must often have regaled the artist with impassioned stories of his mentor's many accomplishments and longstanding efforts on behalf of American blacks.[3]

Though little is known of Woodville's life, he was clearly fascinated by his family's distinguished history. Named after Robert Goodloe

---

3. By no means do I intend my reading of Woodville's *Old '76 and Young '48* to be the painting's definitive interpretation. This beautiful scene was first and foremost a work of fiction, and as such, it can be understood in any number of ways. For descriptions of Woodville's life and art that have influenced my perceptions, see Francis S. Grubar, "Richard Caton Woodville: An American Artist, 1825 to 1855" (Ph.D. Dissertation, Johns Hopkins University, 1966); idem, *Richard Caton Woodville: An Early American Genre Painter* (Washington: Concoran Gallery of Art, 1967); Albert Boime, *The Art of Exclusion: Representing Blacks in the Nineteenth Century* (Washington: Smithsonian Institution Press, 1990), 102-103; Elizabeth Johns, *American Genre Painting: The Politics of Everyday Life* (New Haven: Yale University Press, 1991), 178-82; and Gail E. Husch, "'Freedom's Holy Cause': History, Religious, and Genre Painting in America, 1840-1860," in William S. Ayers, ed., *Picturing History: American Painting, 1770-1930* (New York: Rizzoli International Publications and the Fraunces Tavern Museum, 1993).

FIGURE ELEVEN. *Old '76 and Young '48*. Oil on canvas by Richard Caton Woodville, 1849. Courtesy of the Walters Art Gallery, Baltimore.

Harper's brother–in–law, Woodville frequently used relatives and acquaintances as models for the characters in his paintings. He was, in the words of Bryan Wolf, obsessed with "the theme of generational conflict and reconciliation," and his great–uncle, Richard Caton, was probably the basis for the elderly man on the porch in *War News from Mexico*. Some writers have suggested that Caton may even have been the model for the Revolutionary War veteran in *Old '76 and Young '48*. Yet Caton came to Maryland only after the war with Britain had ended. Woodville would have remembered Harper as the family's most famous military hero.[4]

It is likely that Woodville studied the Harpers' extensive collection of paintings, along with those of other prominent Baltimore families, during the early stages of his artistic training. Viewing one of the General's several portraits at Oakland, perhaps he contemplated how the renowned statesman would have looked were he living then. In the final analysis it matters little whether Woodville really did have Robert Goodloe Harper in mind when he painted *Old '76 and Young '48*. I still see Harper there, sitting by the fire, cane in hand, pondering his own role in slavery's rapid westward expansion.

Today, the family burying grounds are no longer at Oakland. Like Harper's majestic Spring House, which rests peacefully on the lawn adjacent to the Baltimore Museum of Art, the graves were removed years ago to make way for the projects of local developers. Harper's gravestone now adorns the top of a small hill in the middle of Greenmount Cemetery overlooking the poorest regions of Baltimore City. On one side of the monument, a pensive Lady Liberty looks downward. Before her stretches a sea of white markers, separated from the run–down and burned–out houses of the inner city by a jagged stone wall. Even in death, Harper's narrow white world remains hidden behind a barricade, forever segregated from the masses looming ominously outside the cemetery gates.[5]

I do not think Harper would be surprised to behold such poverty and

---

4. Bryan Wolf, "All the World's a Code: Art and Ideology in Nineteenth–Century American Painting," *Art Journal* 44 (Winter 1984): 328-37. Though many have assumed that Richard Caton (1763-1845) was Woodville's grandfather, he was actually the artist's great–uncle. Many scholars and even Woodville's son have confused the genealogy. See especially R. Caton Woodville, Jr., *Random Recollections* (London: Eveleigh Nash, 1914), 9-13.

5. For more information on Harper's dairy, consult William Voss Elder, *Maryland Period Rooms* (Baltimore: Baltimore Museum of Art, 1987), 31; James F. Waesche, *Crowning the Gravelly Hill: A History of the Roland Park–Guilford–Homeland District* (Baltimore: Maclay and Associates, 1987), 13.

FIGURE TWELVE. Harper's Spring House. Designed by Benjamin Latrobe, circa 1812. Originally on the grounds of Oakland, the building was moved to its present site at the Baltimore Museum of Art in 1932. Photograph courtesy of the author.

inequality. Time has proven that in certain respects he was far more realistic about the problems of race and slavery than many abolitionists. Nearly two centuries have passed since his death, and the social conditions of blacks and whites remain far from equal. Nonetheless, one cannot excuse Harper's insensitivity to the evils of slavery and the feelings of African Americans. He was determined to secure his world at their expense. Had Harper attempted to ameliorate the conditions of blacks for their sakes rather than his own, he might have found a means of resolving his moral dilemma. In the end, he was unable to overcome this tragic flaw. On Harper's gravestone opposite Lady Liberty, a Latin inscription reads, "Vir cui ad summam auctoritatem nihil defuit praeter sanam civium mentem": A man who could have obtained the highest honor had only his countrymen been in their right minds.[6]

---

6. The translation of the Latin is my own. For one version that Harper may have read, see Livy, *The History of Rome*, trans. by George Baker (Georgetown: William Fry, 1823), 3: 100. The quotation is from Book XXIII. See also Timothy J. Moore's discussion of Livy's references to wisdom and virtue in Moore, *Artistry and Ideology: Livy's Vocabulary of Virtue* (Frankfurt: Athenaeum, 1989), 107-20.

FIGURE THIRTEEN. A view from the grave. Photograph courtesy of the author.

FIGURE FOURTEEN. Harper's gravestone. Designed by John H. B. Latrobe. Photograph courtesy of the author.

APPENDICES

A.

"A discourse on Learning"*

——————...•..——————

ADISCOURSE delivered at Cambridge March 15.th 1788. the first Anniversary of the Cambridge friendly Society for the encouragement of Literature—By the direction of the Society, and written out afterwards at their request.

As this day was set apart for celebrating the anniversary of the Cambridge friendly society for the encouragement of Literature, it was thought expedient by the members that something should be said in public on the nature and design of the institution; when this had been resolved, we immediately turned our eyes on the gentleman whose learning and abilities qualify him best for expatiating on the benefits of Liberal education, and explaining the means by which it may be promoted: but he having declined to gratify our wishes, the task was laid on me, that the public expectation might not be intirely disappointed.

Since such is the occasion of our meeting, before I speak of the causes which render the means of instruction scarce & of difficult attainment among us, and of the remedy for these inconveniences which this institution is calculated to afford, I hope it will not be thought improper to enlarge a little on the advantages of learning in general, and the particular benefits which individuals and communities may derive from the good education of youth. If in doing this I should be carried unawares beyond the limits which modesty and the diffidence suitable to my years seem to prescribe, I hope I may be pardoned. No subject is so apt to fire the mind of a speaker; none so beautiful and important; none so copious;

---

* The manuscript version of this document is owned by Ms. Carolyn T. Fisher, a Harper descendant living in Towson, Maryland. A microfilm copy of the original is available through interlibrary loan from the Maryland State Archives [MSA M7268]. The transcript that follows preserves Harper's spelling and punctuation. Brackets denote additions made for the sake of clarity, and ellipses have been placed wherever Harper accidentally repeated a word or phrase.

none in which out of the great number of things that may be said it is so difficult to select what is alone suitable to the speaker, the audience and the occasion.

The great and beneficial effects—which learning tends to produce, are the improvement of the mind, the amendment of the heart, and the advancement of rational and true religion.

Our minds like our bodies, and like all the productions of nature, are weak and helpless in their infant state, but as they grow towards maturity they encrease in strength in activity and in hardiness, and their improvement in any of these particulars, is always in proportion to their exercise. A person who from infancy to manhood has been accustomed to lift great weights, and to spend much of his time in laborious employments, will possess far greater strength, and be much more capable of sustaining fatigues and hardship, than one who has spent his life in idleness or in sedintary occupations. Take two young horses of equal blood and equal beauty, let one be exercised in leaping and running; neglect the other, or employ him in drawing a cart, and how greatly will the former excell in swiftness and agility? Thus also the infant mind is improved by exercise and that exercise learning supplies. Learning increases its powers, and strengthens its faculties by engaging them in frequent and vigorous exertions. The Memory, the Judgment, the Fancy, the Invention, are all kept in constant employment, which improves them no less than swiftness is improved by frequent running, or strength by the constant practice of wrestling. By this exercise of the mind they who have been instructed in learning from their early years obtain a superiority in mental endowments far greater than others possess in bodily powers; Compare a human creature in the lowest with one in the highest state of improvement, and how vast will the distance between them appear! Can we imagine one being more superior to another than a Franklin a Witherspoon, or a Jefferson, to a negro just landed from the Coast of Africa? Yet these creatures are of the same species; they came into the world in all respects alike, except in the colour of their skin, and the difference between them, great as it appears, arises wholly from education. The former have received the highest cultivation of which human nature is capable; and they shine with the brightest rays of mental excellence; the latter from his infancy destitute of the least cultivation still grovels in the same darkness ignorance and meanness which accompanied him into the world. If we examine the various degrees which lie between these extremes of mental weakness & perfection, we shall find that they are in exact proportion to the various degrees of instruction which the different classes of men have obtained. The negro who landed yesterday has been wholly destitute of any the least instruction; he is accordingly at the lowest point of ignorance and baseness. He eats, he sleeps, from the instruments of nature: his mind is wholly vacant; his recollection does not reach back as far as yesterday; his foresight does not extend to tomorrow: he seems to sink down almost to a level with the brute creation, and in some things appears even inferior to some of the brutes. His countryman who has been ten years among us, has been reduced indeed during all that time to the most abject slavery; but he has enjoyed some small scraps of instruction, his faculties have been accustomed to a little more exertion, and some faint glimmerings of knowledge have pervaded his mind. He therefore is much superior to him who landed but yesterday. The Negro who was born or brought up among us from his earliest years, is superior to both the former because he has enjoyed still greater means of instruction than they, and has caught from his masters some tincture of improvement. The poor labouring white man, who in his infancy or child hood learned to read, to scrawl his name, and to perform some of the plainer rules of arithmetic, and whose mind has since been sometimes exercised by reflecting on his own little affairs [ranks even higher than these classes of negroes] because the instruction which he has enjoyed, though extremely limited, is yet far greater than theirs. Above the labourer rises the merchant and man of business, whose early instruction has been greater, and whose mind is more improved by the exercise it finds in arranging & settling accounts, and in conducting affairs which require more frequent reflection and a greater extent of thought. The next degree of mental excellence is possessed by the gentle-man of liberal education and affluence or easy fortune. He has enjoyed more leasure and more abundant means of instruction than the mere man of business: Study however has been not his employment, but his recreation; business and pleasure have occupied a larger portion of his time. He is therefore superior to the mere man of business, but inferior to the schollar the man of science the Philosopher; who holds the most distinguished rank in the mental world, because his opportunities of improvement have been equal to his wishes, and it has been the business and the pleasure of his life to cultivate his mind, to enlarge its powers, and to fill it with the richest stores of knowledge and sentiment. Such once were Aristotle, Plato, Tully, Bacon, Locke, Newton & Montesquieu; and such at this day are Franklin, Jefferson, Witherspoon, and Maddison. Thus we see that Education, bestowing improvements on some, which are withheld from others, creates the vast difference we percieve in the degrees of mental excellence. Education sets the negro who has been ten years in America above him who has landed but yesterday, and gives him who was born among us a superiority over both; education sets the labourer above the highest class of negroes, the man of business above the labourer, the gentleman of liberal education above both the former, and raises the Philosopher above them all. I know that there are some particular instances which seem to contradict this opinion. We sometimes see men unaded by education rise to great destinction by the native strength and richness of their genius; while others in attempts to instruct whom much care has been employed, still remain ignorant & stupid. But still it is true that education gives a vast superiority. If the man who without the aid of mental improvement has obtained distinction by the...inborn force of his genius, had enjoyed the advantages which learning can bestow, how much more illustrious would his talents have appeared! on the other hand had he whom not education itself could rescue from ignorance and dulness, been deprived of that help, into what a gulph of stupidity must [he] have sunk!

This improvement of mind thus bestowed by learning extends its utility to every department of public and private life. By the various accidents and changes in human affairs, all other possessions may be lost. The Merchant to day sees himself possessed of thousands; a storm arises and to morrow all his wealth lies at the bottom of the ocean. A fire breaks out in a town, and numbers whom Yesterdays sun saw living in affluence or splendor, are now reduced to poverty. War sweeps away our cattle and our slaves; fatal seasons destroy our crops; exile or imprisonment may deprive us of our fortunes, our friends, and our famalies. But the treasures of learning no accident can destroy, no violence snatch from us, no fraud steal away. They will go with us into banishment, accompany us in prison ships, escape with us from the flames which devour our possessions, and swim out with us from shipwreck. In the course of life it happens more or less to all of us to be sometimes left alone, when we are prevented from applying to business, and can obtain no amusement. How irksome are such hours to the illiterate man! how heavily do they hang on his hands! his vacant mind incapable of any but course and sensual enjoyments, often flies to scenes of noise and riot and senseless mirth, to escape from the fatigue of idleness and solitude. But to a mind adorned with learning these are the sweetest and most precious moments of life. With what eagerness does it catch at such happy hours! with what delight does it withdraw from the bustle of business, & escape from the interruption of company, to give itself up to the most refined and noble pleasures! Then we enjoy ourselves; then we converse with our own hearts, recollect our own conduct & try to amend whatever is wrong in our dispositions and behavior, and reflect on the conduct of others, that we may avoid their faults and imitate their virtues; then we converse with the most illustrious men of every age, grow enamoured of their characters, and endeavour to form our hearts by the example of their virtue; then we make ourselves more fit to discharge the duties of this...life, prepare ourselves for the life to come. For these reasons one of the greatest and best men of any age, used to declare that he was never less idle than when he had nothing to do, nor ever less alone than when he had no company. These are the pleasures, these the advantages which learning enables us to obtain in retirement and solitude! who then would not wish to possess it if it could bestow no other benefit? One of our most common complaints is the shortness of life, yet short as it is, all that portion of it which is not devoted to business, a considerable part of every mans, and almost the whole of some mens time, is spent by the illiterate in idleness or something worse. All these hours are, in a manner, voids in their time, in which they cannot be said to live. These voids learning enables us to fill up, and thereby to remidy the shortness of life. Certainly if life were to be measured, as it ought to be, by those hours only which we employ in some useful or realy agreeable purpose, it would be found that a studious man of letters, in the same number of years, had lived at least twice as long as the vulgar and illiterate. The improvement derived from learning procures also respect and weight among our neighbours, our acquaintance, and in the world. When a man of sense, whose mind has been cultivated by a good education, engages in private conversation or public debates, with what respect is he heard! What difference do men pay his judgment! how willing are they to be governed by his advice in their private concerns, and to trust their public affairs to his management! What can be more honourable than to excel others in that which all men wish chiefly to possess! I mean understanding & knowledge. What can add greater ornament & dignity to a character than the reputation of superior sense? What can be more flattering than such a preeminence? Men are pleased with excelling others in strength, in swiftness and in activity; and even this superiority gives some ornament to those who possess it. But after the utmost we can attain, the dog will excead us in activity, the ox in strength, and the horse in swiftness. If then a preiminence be desireable, in that which beasts possess in a higher degree than we can ever hope to attain, how glorious must it be to excel in mental endowments which argues a nature above the rest of our species, and raises us one degree nearer to superior beings? To discern the power of learning in enabling us to raise a fortune and obtain distinction in public life, we need only cast our eyes on the bar, the bench, and the house of assembly. How many do we see there who having received from their fathers no other patrimony than a good education, now possess competent or affluent fortunes, and occupy the most distinguished posts in public affairs? Who without education can expect to obtain a seat on the bench, or hope for eminence at the bar? What but education can give a man that superior influence in the legislature which unites in his single person the opinions and votes of the whole body, and enables him to inform their minds, direct their judgment, & dictate their proceedings? These are powers and advantages, which not birth, connections, wealth, nothing but the endowments of the mind can bestow. They also bestow others, less illustrious perhaps, but by no means inconsiderable. What occupation can be more honourable than to preside over the education of youth? What can be a more comfortable provision for life than the emoluments of that profession? This is a business for which learning only can render us fit, and he that is qualified for it, has obtained a provision for life, more valuable because less uncertain, than any estate: a provision which will be ready when other resources fail; Which cannot be taken from him by accident fraud or open violence. In former times some merchants with a ship richly laden were going on a trading voyage, and they had on board a philosopher famous in that age for his learning & genius. A storm arose. The ship was wrecked on an unknown coast. The rich cargo went to the bottom. The merchants, the crew, and the Philosopher swam naked to the shore, and landed among strangers; where destitute of friends and of credit, they were in danger of starving. The philosopher however soon made himself known, and was employed in instructing the youth of the place. By this he procured necessaries for himself and the companions of his misfortune, and in a short time was able to furnish them with the means of returning to their own country. What a striking instance of the advantage of learning! the wealth of the merchants sunk in the sea: the philosopher's learning swam with him to shore: there it supported them in their extreme distress, when not all their former riches could protect them from hunger and cold. But Learning does more than enabling us to procure wealth honours, and happiness for ourselves; it qualifies us to serve others; to serve our friends; our fellow citizens, our country and mankind: to improve their minds, form their manners, mend their hearts, explain and defend their rights, and promote their happiness. This is the noble and distinguished use of mental endowments; this is the employment most honourable, and worthy of a man. The beasts are careful only about themselves, but it becomes man to extend his care to others, and to labour for the happiness of his fellow creatures. How frequently does a man of well cultivated mind find opportunities of communicating knowledge to those with whom he converses! of imparting useful instruction to the youth of his acquaintance, of sowing the seeds of knowledge in their minds, of inflaming them with the desire of improvement, and assisting them to obtain it; of instiling just noble, and generous principles into their hearts by his conversation, & forming their manners to propriety, and politeness by his example! The knowledge of such a man, like a public library, becomes a common property; his conversation, like a spring shower, enriches wherever it falls; his character is a model which all may imitate with advantage; his house and his table are schools for good manners, and mental improvement. If his circumstances be narrow, he still may do much good; if his fortune be large, it enables him to diffuse more widely the benefits of his mind. How frequently might such a man become the arbiter of differences between his neighbours, and acquaintances. The weight which his superior knowledge would give him, would often put it in his power to settle their disputes, to determine their rights, and persuade them to acquiesce in equitable compromises. We are all in our turn called to serve on juries. There we must pass sentence on the property, often on the life of our fellow citizens. Points of dark and difficult proof are submitted to our determination. We are required to weigh the various degrees of probability in contradicting witnesses, and to build up a full proof from confused & broken materials: and the utmost art of learned and ingenious pleaders is often exerted to overcloud the truth, & to perplex & mislead our judgment. Nothing but the attention of mind, the discernment, and quickness of apprehension derived from learning, or at least greatly improved by it, can enable us to perceive the truth in these difficult circumstances, and keep close to justice in our determinations. Many of us are appointed [to] execute the laws, and to preside in courts as magistrates; and in the discharge of both these functions, their determinations essentially affect the property & persons of their fellow citizens. The improvement of mind derived from learning enables them to understand clearly the principles of law, and gives them those just and comprehensive notions of equity, by which their conduct ought to be directed. What important benefits does learning enable a man to confer on the public by the education of youth. To train up the rising generation in virtue, sense, and knowledge; to give them the qualifications which adorn humanity, & inspire them with those sentiments which do honour to our nature, and procure for such as are actuated by them, the veneration of mankind, are some of the services which learning enables [a man] this way to render to individuals and the community. Learning is also a necessary qualification in a minister of religion. This is among the most useful, the most honourable & the most important stations of life, and it cannot be filled without mental improvement. Can any thing be a more lasting, or a more important benefit to the Community than to instil the principles of piety and duty into the hearts of the people, to frighten them from vice by painting its deformity and destructive consequences, and allure them to virtue by convincing them of its beauty, its excellence, and its happy effects? In fine to teach them a religion which by the fear of punishments and the hope of rewards, may restrain them from crimes, and make them better citizens and better men? In the legislature, in Congress, the necessity of a well cultivated mind is so obvious that it needs no illustration. Without the endowments of the mind, a man in those important stations is useless at best, often he is pernicious. Incapable of comprehending the reason of measures, or discerning their tendency, he is often made the tool of other mens policy; often promotes wicked measures, which perhaps, if he understood them, he would detest. But to discover the tendency of other mens schemes; to discern with clearness and certainty, what is hurtful to the public, and oppose it with success; to set on foot beneficial measures ourselves, or to support and carry them into effect when brought forward by others; to watch over the public safety like a skilful general watches over his army in an enemies country, and to guard against every, even the most remote, chance of danger, are some of the services which mental improvement enables a man to render his Country, in those high stations. As an Ambassador in foreign courts, it enables him to perform services still more important: To discover at a distance, and avoid an approaching war; to discern the strengths, dispositions, views, and interests, of various powers, and to conduct his measures as these demand; to engage other nations in the protection of his country, by their policy, their pride, and their mutual jealousy; to place the balance of their various interests in the hands of his country, and to obtain for it some solid commercial advantage from their negotiations, their jealousies, and their quarels.

Thus view man in every department of life; take him in a public or a private station, whether we consider him as an individual or a member of society; with reference to himself, or in his relations to others; mental improvement enables him to obtain and confer, lasting happiness & solid advantages.

Did learning produce no other effect than this improvement of the mind; did it bestow no other advantage than the power of doing good, of serving ourselves and promoting the happiness of others, it would be glorious and desirable indeed, but often useless, sometimes pernicious. We might have the power of doing good, but the will would [be] wanting: the understanding might be cultivated, but the heart cold and depraved. But learning also warms and enables the heart. Learning implants in the breast the love of virtue, and inspires us with benevolence, disinterestedness and public spirit. The force of example in forming the heart, especially in early years, is universally known. How desirous are we in childhood and youth to imitate what we hear commended in others? How naturally do we admire actions which have done honour to the authors of them, and procured for the...love, the admiration and the applauses of the world! With what veneration and delight do we reflect on characters whose virtues all nations, have united in admiring loving and extolling! How deep, and how lasting are the impressions made in early years, while the heart is tender and sincere, untainted with vice, not yet chilled and frozen by views of sordid interest, a stranger to little selfish passions, and easily susceptible of whatever is noble, generous and excellent! Learning sets before the youthful mind numberless examples of the most illustrious virtue; being it acquainted with the most distinguished characters of former ages, whose virtues were the light, the boast, and the admiration of the times they lived in, the honour of their country, & the ornament of human nature, and whose persons were the delight of their friends their country, and of mankind. Learning raises these illustrious persons from their tombs, introduces us early into their company, and enables us at all times to enjoy their conversation. She makes us imbibe their principles, catch the fire of virtue and patriotism from their souls, and by constantly reminding us of their rewards, their praises and the lustre of their names, inspires us with an ardent wish to imitate their conduct. It has often been said that virtue is in herself so amiable, that to make us love her, we need but be seen. Learning shows her in her most beautiful form; shining with untainted lustre in prosperity; rising superiour to the rudest shocks of adversity; adorned with the veneration, the love, and the admiration of mankind. Precepts, though less efficacious than example in forming the heart, are yet of great force when applied in early life, frequently inculcated, and conveyed in a pleasing manner. How naturally do we imbibe notions in early life which we frequently hear repeated and always admitted as true! They often grow into our dispositions, and influence our conduct through future life. It is then of the greatest importance that the precepts which we receive in infancy and youth, be such as inculcate virtue. How much do our future conduct our character, and our happiness depend on what we learn at that age! Early learning inculcates from our infancy the most sublime precepts of justice temperance, magninimity, public spirit, gratitude, and benevolence: it accustoms us to hear them every day, to have them constantly in our thoughts to repeat them continually, and gradually to engraft on them our sentiments and opinions. Formal instruction, and sett lessons, are distasteful and tiresome to young minds; but they listen eagerly to agreeable conversation, and quickly imbibe what they frequently hear repeated in company. Learning introduces us into the company of the wise and virtuous of every age. We hear their discourses, and drink in from their lips the precepts of virtue. Their conversation adorned with all the graces of language and thought, captivates our taste, and while it engages our attention by its beauty, insensibly sends to the heart the principles of virtue. Since the maxims which we are early accustomed to hear make so deep an impression, and have such decisive influence...in forming our dispositions and character, it is of the utmost importance that we should be taught as early as possible to examine them and Judge of their truth. Many of the principles which the world takes for granted, and which are constantly in the mouths of some people, are no less false than destructive in their tendency. Many rules of conduct are laid down and practised in our days which are extremely hostile to the good of society. Such for instance, as these, that the chief attention of every one ought to be employed about money; that nothing is dishonest which the laws do not punish; that provided we can take care of ourselves, no matter what becomes of others; that no person is obliged to give up his own advantage for the public benefit or safety; that it is proper to screen our friend from punishment, though they be guilty of the most flagitious crimes; that poverty is dishonourable, and honest labour a disgrace; that it is better to be rich by any means whatsoever, than to be poor with a good conscience and an upright character; that happiness consists in wealth; that virtue is a matter of convenience, and religion a thing of little consequence; that a future state of rewards and punishments is a vain notion; that God pays little attention to the affairs of the world; these and many other notions equally false, & equally pernicious, are very commonly received in our times. Learning by strengthening our minds, by giving us habits of reflection and enquiry, enables us to examine these opinions, to discover their falsity and danger, and to reject them. It enables us to discern that happiness consists in virtue and is wholly independent on fortune; that duty is at all times to be preferred to interest or convenience; that it is more glorious to serve others than to employ our whole care about ourselves; that the advantage of individuals should at all times be sacrificed to the public benefit; that the silent approbation of our own minds is always to be preferred to honours, riches, and the applauses of others; that honest poverty is better than guilty wealth; that riches when improperly acquired, or improperly used, are a curse; that it is not lawful to practice injustice for our own advantage, or that of our friends, even when we could do it without danger of punishment or shame; that God will certainly at some time, or in some way or other, punish such as wilfully violate his laws; that future, and even present, happiness, will be the reward of such as spend their lives in the practise duty), and in cultivating virtuous dispositions. These are the truths which learning enables us to discover, and allures us to practice by a conviction of their importance. How favourable are these truths to virtue! What happy effects would the practice of them produce in public and private! How greatly would it promote the happiness of individuals and the good of states! These are the means by which learning forms the heart to virtue. It works by the most powerful methods of instruction; by example, by precepts, and by reasoning. The utility of virtue in every circumstance, and situation of life, is extremely obvious. If fortune smile on us, virtue adds lustre dignity and ornament to our character. If misfortunes assail us from without, or afflictions from within, virtue enables us to retire within ourselves, to rise superior to adversity, and support ourselves upon the firm prop of an approving conscience. Caesar vanquished his opposers, triumphed over the liberties of his Country, and made himself lord of the world; but Caesar had not virtue, and he was miserable amidst the homage of mankind. Caesar drove Marcellus into banishment, murdered his friends, and seized his possessions; the virtue of Marcellus accompanied him in exile, and made him serene and happy in the midst of poverty afflictions, and public Calamities. To a mind devoid of virtue how dreadful is the recollection of the past, how fearful the prospect of the future! with what horror does it fly from solitude and reflection! how do the stings of conscience encrease the pains of sickness! How fearful is a death bed! In these awful moments, light company, mirth and noise, his usual protectors from thought no longer assist him: they forsake him and leave him a prey to painful recollections and gloomy forebodings; But the virtuous man reflects on the past with a sweet complacency and looks forward with a well grounded hope to the future. The approbation of his own mind supports him in sickness, and the recollection of a well spent life deprives death of its terrors. How serene, how bright, how beautiful, are his last moments! let me die the death of the righteous, and let my last end be like his, was the prayer of Balaam: come said Mr. Addison to his friends, a few moments before he expired, come and see with what composure a Christian can die. Why do you weep said the divine Socrates after he had drank the poison, to his disconsolate friends, as if I had suffered some great calamity: My enemies could not kill me without the permission of the Gods, and are you grieved to see me who have spent my life in doing their will, obey it also in dying? Believe me if they had not greater happiness in store for me in another life, they would permit me to remain longer here. How ornamental, how useful, how necessary is virtue in public stations! What dignity what weight does it give to private characters! Mental improvement gives us power to serve our friends, our country and mankind; virtue inclines us to exert that power. Who without virtue will exert himself in the public service! will sacrifice his ease and his private advantage, to the good of his Country? will divest himself of all sordid

selfish views, & resist the temptations of interest, the seductions of ambition, and the influence of party? Acknowledged virtue adds greatly to the
power of doing good, by the weight it gives to a mans opinion, and the
personal influence he derives form it. How many do we see, who not
remarkable for their talents, and often unaided by learning obtain from
their reputation for integrity great influence in private, & authority in
public concerns? If so sordid a motive as the making of a fortune, might
be mentioned among the advantages of virtue, it is obvious that it affords
us great assistance in that pursuit. A man of know[n] integrity has the
assistance and confidence of all; every one is willing to trust him; and his
credit often enables him to seize opportunities of improving his fortune,
which others cannot use without money. Colonel Chartres, the most
finished rascal perhaps that ever was born, once declared that he would
give fifty thousand pounds for the reputation of a certain man's virtue.
Not that I care for virtue said he, or wish to possess the reputation of it;
but because such a character as that man enjoys, would soon enable me to
gain an hundred thousand. If a virtuous man happen to be overborne by
misfortune, all pity him, all wish to see him rise, and to favour his
exertions. By this assistance he is often enabled to retrieve his affairs, and
to extricate himself from difficulties, under which any man must have
sunk, who had not the support of an upright character. Virtue in fine, is
useful in private & necessary in public life, and it adds ornament and
dignity to every circumstance and situation. It is the parent, the nurse of
religion, [that] paves the way for her entrance and prepares the heart for
her reception. But Learning introduces and fixes her in the heart; learning
enlightens her and gives her that solid foundation and liberal cast, which
distinguish rational and true religion, from low superstition, bigottry and
furious zeal. Dean Swift who was perfectly acquainted with the world, in
speaking of free thinkers declares that he never knew any person of
liberal education and regular morals, who professed himself to be of that
class. The belief of a god, of his being, perfections, and providence; the
immortality of the soul, and a future state of rewards and punishments;
are the groundworks of true religion. The illiterate man recieves these
great truths upon trust; he assents to them because he has been always
accustomed to hear them; but he neither examines, or comprehends the
reasons on which they are founded. But the man of science believes these
truths not like uncertain reports, because he has heard them, but because
he has seen them, and sees them every day, and every hour. He sees them

in every part of the creation; in the sun, the stars, the clouds, the earth and its productions, the change of seasons, the revolution of day and night. The frame of his body, the constitution of his nature, and the operations of his mind: he hears them in the awful voice of thunder, in the bellowing of the ocean, & feels them in the uncontrolable fury of the winds. The illiterate man walks abroad amidst all these wonders, without their once attracting his notice. By seeing them every day from his birth he has become habituated to them and treats them like common objects. He goes on beholding them till his death without once reflecting on their grandeur, their beauty, or their usefulness: without comprehending or enquiring after, their nature, their causes, or the laws by which they are supported and governed. The man of liberal knowledge on the contrary views them with perpetual wonder delight and reverence; he finds in them the clearest and most convincing proof of a god, of his providence, power, wisdom and goodness; of his justice, of the necessity of obeying his laws, and of the immortality of rational beings. Hence he has a fuller & stronger conviction of these great truths, which therefore operate more powerfully in directing his actions, and forming his character. It is often and most truly observed that ignorance is the parent of presumpsion; when we know a little, we are most apt to think highly of our own capacity and attainments; and if we once come to believe that we are capable of knowing and comprehending every thing, it is an infalible proof that we know but very little indeed. Hence we see so many shallow coxcombs, abundantly wise in their own conceit, who go about raising cavils against religion, calling in question the truth of revelation, and pretending to prove that virtue and morality are idle notions, that man is incapable of resisting his passions, and came into the world for the purpose of gratifying them in their fullest extent. They find something in religion morality and providence, which they cannot comprehend, and they wisely conclude that their is no such thing: just as if a mole should take on himself to prove that there is no sun, because he cannot see it, or discern the difference between it and a candle. They find fault with all the works of God, and imagine that things would have been better ordered, had they been consulted at the creation. This astonishing presumption, which however is so common in our times that it almost ceases to surprise us, can arise from nothing but the most profound ignorance and blindness. But liberal learning opens our eyes. It makes us discover how limited is the human capacity, how weak the human mind, how dark human reason. It informs us that the mind of man in its most improved and exalted State, cannot explain a thousand objects which every moment present themselves to our attention: cannot tell why leaves grow on the trees, and grass springs from the ground, why the seeds of any plant when put into the earth, will produce the same plant again; why fishes cannot live out of the water, nor beasts in it; why fire consumes wood and melts metals; cannot explain the least motion we make with our limbs, the least sound we produce with our tongues, nor the reason why our senses when affected by external objects, present ideas of those objects to our minds each in a different way; why we do not see with our ears, hear with our palates, and taste with our fingers ends; nor what that power is which brings a stone back to the earth, after it has been thrown into the air. These are the most common objects of nature; we have them perpetually before our eyes. Yet these things the man of learning finds that he cannot comprehend. Will he then censure the conduct of the most high, or call in question the propriety of his decrees? No! he will study his works to find out his will, not to propose amendments, he will sometimes with humility and diffidence examine his nature and his laws; but he will oftener, wonder believe, and adore. When religion takes possession of weak and unenlightened minds, it is extremely apt to degenerate to low superstition, or bigottry. Hence we see multitudes believing that they shall merit the favour of God by observing some unmeaning or ridiculous ceremonies, while they perpetually neglect or infringe his laws. Hence we see some individuals, and sects, condemning others to eternal misery, because they hold or reject some misterious, or uninteligible doctrines, or because they worship the same God with different rites, or performed the same rites, in a different way from themselves. But learning enlightens our minds, & enables us to reject these unworthy prejudices, and destructive errors. It enables us to offer up such a prayer as this. Lord I know not whether we ought to pray to thee standing, sitting or kneeling. I know not whether the bread used in thy sacrament ought to be broken or cut; I know not whether baptism, the seal of admission into thy church, ought to be afforded to infants, or deferred to riper years, or whether it ought to be performed by marking the water on the forehead in form of a cross, sprinkling it on the face, or plunging the whole body into the water. I know not whether it be more acceptable to sing in thy worship songs composed two thousand years ago, or those that have been written only an hundred. I know not whether thou desirest us to eat the flesh of sheep and oxen, rather than that of hogs or hares. But I know from thy works and from the revelations which thou hast been pleased to make of thyself, that thou art wise just and merciful. I know that the service which thou most desirest, is the performance of thy will, and I have a well grounded hope that the sincere and humble attempts of thy creatures will be accepted. Thou hast enabled us to discover much of thy will; if we perform this to the utmost of our power, should more be necessary, I know that when prayed to with humility and reverence thou wilt reveal it. These are the religious sentiments which learning tends to inspire and cherish by giving us clearer and more lively conceptions of the great truths of morality; by convincing us of our weakness and the blindness of our minds, and thus filling our hearts with reverence humility and adoration; and by lifting us above low and dark superstition.

Thus various, extensive and universal are the benefits of Learning; thus does it improve the mind, implant virtue in the heart, and promote true religion. The want of this copious, this beautiful gift among us, is acknowledged by all; all acknowledge that the means of obtaining it are rare and difficult, difficult to far the greater part, inaccessible to many. To bestow it on those to whom fortune has denied the means of obtaining it, and to render its access easier to all, are the ends for which the society, whose anniversary we now celebrate, was founded. To raise a fund for these purposes each member at his admittance is required to pay the sum of one Dollar, and afterwards an annual contribution of fourteen Shillings. These contributions are small it is true, but so are our fortunes. We are unable to contribute large sums generally; But should any wealthy member be disposed to a noble generosity in advancing our fund, we shall receive his bounty with thanks and gratitude. However these sums though small, if properly managed may in time, produce great effects. When the Society's fund becomes sufficiently large, it is to be put out to interest and the annual produce of it to be applied in hiring teachers for our public school, repairing or enlarging the buildings, purchasing books and other things necessary for study, but above all in supporting at school, such poor lads whose good disposition and genius, fit them to be one day, with the advantage of good education the honour, the or[na]-ment, and the able servants of their country. The Society has weekly meetings on any Saturday when five members are disposed to assemble for that purpose. In these meeting members may be elected, for which purpose they must apply by letter addressed to the society; and other business transacted. It has also quarterly meeting for more important concerns; and yearly meetings to celebrate the anniversary of the society. At these various meetings the company of every member is wished for, but there are no fines or other compulsions. They who contribute to the support of an institution founded for purposes so useful and so honour-able, will have the satisfaction to reflect that they have taken part in conferring a benefit on the community which will extend to future ages. Few of us can serve our country in exalted stations, as lawgivers, as Magistrates or as Generals: but here a way is opened by [which] all may promote more or less the public good. What service to the public so important as to promote learning by which man is lifted from the brutes and placed but a little lower than the angels! by which society is polished, and life refined; by which the mind is improved and the heart corrected; which enables us to serve ourselves, and benefit our country. This is the most laudable; this the most noble use of wealth; a use which will not be confined to ourselves, our own acquain[tan]ce, or our own times; but will defuse its benefits, on the whole community and extend them to the latest ages.

⸌ Finis

B.

Letter to Elias B. Caldwell[*]

———————·••··———————

Baltimore, August 20th, 1817.

DEAR SIR,

Ever since I received your letter of July 11th, requesting the communication of such ideas as had occurred to me, concerning the proposed plan of colonizing the free blacks in the United States, with their own consent, and indeed from the time of our short interview at Washington, when you first mentioned the subject to me, I have kept it constantly in view, and revolved it much in my mind. Hitherto, however, I have been prevented from putting my thoughts on paper, or even digesting and reducing them to method, by various interruptions, arising in part from accident, and in part from professional engagements, in the midst of which I am obliged at last to write. This may interfere very much with the order of my ideas, but will not I trust occasion any material omission. Nor do I apprehend much inconvenience from the delay; since the preparatory measures for the first step in this great enterprise, the institution of a mission to the south western coast of Africa, to explore the ground, and seek out a suitable situation for the establishment of the colony, are not yet I believe entirely completed.

Although you confine your request to the communication of my ideas, concerning the manner and means of accomplishing this great design, it will not I trust be improper or unseasonable, to throw out by way of preface and introduction, some hints on its usefulness and practicability; which have long engaged my attention, and are susceptible I think of very full proof. To many, and especially to you, this I know is quite unnecessary; but great numbers of our countrymen including many persons of good sense considerable influence and best intentions, may

---

[*] Originally published as *A Letter from Gen. Harper, of Maryland, to Elias B. Caldwell, Esq., Secretary of the American Society for Colonizing the Free People of Colour, in the United States, with Their Own Consent* (Baltimore: R. J. Matchett for E. J. Cole, 1818).

have serious doubts on these two points, which it is of great importance to remove, in order to gain their zealous cooperation. Towards the attainment of so desirable an object I wish to contribute my mite, for which this seems to be a fit occasion.

In reflecting on the utility of a plan for colonizing the free people of colour, with whom our country abounds, it is natural that we should be first struck by its tendency to confer a benefit on ourselves, by ridding us of a population for the most part idle and useless, and too often vicious and mischievous. These persons are condemned to a state of hopeless inferiority and degradation, by their colour; which is an indelible mark of their origin and former condition, and establishes an impassible barrier between them and the whites. This barrier is closed for ever, by our habits and our feelings, which perhaps it would be more correct to call our prejudices; and which, whether feelings or prejudices, or a mixture of both, make us recoil with horror from the idea of an intimate union with the free blacks, and preclude the possibility of such a state of equality between them and us, as alone could make us one people. Whatever justice humanity and kindness we may feel towards them, we cannot help considering them and treating them as our inferiors; nor can they help viewing themselves in the same light, however hard and unjust they may be inclined to consider such a state of things. We cannot help associating them, in our feelings and conduct, nor can they help in associating themselves, with the slaves, who have the same colour, the same origin, and the same manners, and with whom they or their parents have been recently in the same condition. Be their industry ever so great and their conduct ever so correct, whatever property they may acquire, or whatever respect we may feel for their characters, we never could consent, and they never could hope, to see the two races placed on a footing of perfect equality with each other: to see the free blacks or their descendants visit in our houses, form part of our circle of acquaintance, marry into our families, or participate in public honours and employments. This is strictly true of every part of our country, even those parts where slavery has long ceased to exist, and is held in abhorrence. There is no state in the union, where a negro or mulatto can ever hope to be a member of congress, a judge, a militia officer, or even a justice of the peace: to sit down at the same table with the respectable whites, or to mix freely in their society. I may safely assert that Paul Cuffe, respectable intelligent and wealthy as he is, has no expectation or chance of ever being invited to dine with any gentleman in Boston, of marrying his daughter, whatever may be her fortune or education, to one of their sons, or of seeing his son obtain a wife among their daughters.

This circumstance, arising from the difference of colour and origin between the slaves and the free class, distinguishes the slavery of America from that of every other country, ancient or modern. Slavery existed among almost all the ancient nations. It now exists throughout Asia, Africa and America, and in every part of the Russian and Turkish dominions in Europe: that is in more than three–fourths of the world. But the great body of the slaves, every where except in North and South America, are of the same race origin colour and general character with the free people. So it was among the ancients. Manumission, therefore, by removing the slave from the condition of slavery, exempted him from its consequences, and opened his way to a full participation in all the benefits of freedom. He was raised to an equality with the free class, became incorporated into it with his family, and might by good fortune, or good conduct, soon wash out the stain, and obliterate the remembrance, of his former degraded condition.

But in the United States this is impossible. You may manumit the slave, but you cannot make him a white man. He still remains a negro or a mulatto. The mark and the recollection of his origin and former state still adhere to him; the feelings produced by that condition, in his own mind and in the minds of the whites, still exist; he is associated by his colour, and by these recollections and feelings, with the class of slaves; and a barrier is thus raised between him and the whites, that is between him and the free class, which he can never hope to transcend. With the hope he gradually loses the desire. The debasement which was at first compulsory, has now become habitual and voluntary. The incitement to good conduct and exertion, which arises from the hope of raising himself or his family in the world, is a stranger to his breast. He looks forward to no distinction, aims at no excellence, and makes no effort beyond the supply of his daily wants; and the restraints of character being lost to him, he seeks, regardless of the future, to obtain that supply, by the means which cost him the least present trouble. The authority of the master being removed, and its place not being supplied by moral restraints or incitements, he lives in idleness, and probably in vice, and obtains a precarious support by begging or theft. If he should avoid these extremes, and follow some regular course of industry, still the habits of thoughtless improvidence which he contracted while a slave himself, or has caught from the slaves among whom he is forced to live, who of necessity are his companions and associates, prevent him from making any permanent provision for his support, by prudent foresight and economy; and in case of sickness, or of bodily disability from any other cause, send him to live as a pauper, at the expense of the community.

There are, no doubt, many honourable and some very distinguished exceptions; but I may safely appeal to the observation of every man, at all acquainted with the class of people in question, for the correctness of this picture.

Such a class must evidently be a burden and a nuisance to the community; and every scheme which affords a prospect of removing so great an evil, must deserve to be most favourably considered.

But it is not in themselves merely that the free people of colour are a nuisance and burden. They contribute greatly to the corruption of the slaves, and to aggravate the evils of their condition, by rendering them idle discontented and disobedient. This also arises from the necessity under which the free blacks are, of remaining incorporated with the slaves, of associating habitually with them, and forming part of the same class in society. The slave seeing his free companion live in idleness, or subsist, however scantily or precariously, by occasional desultory employment, is apt to grow discontented with his own condition, and to regard as tyranny and injustice the authority which compels him to labour. Hence he is strongly incited to elude this authority, by neglecting his work as much as possible, to withdraw himself from it altogether by flight, and sometimes to attempt direct resistance. This provokes or impels the master to a severity, which would not otherwise by thought necessary; and that severity, by rendering the slave still more discontented with his lot, and more hostile towards his master, by adding the sentiments of resentment and revenge to his original dissatisfaction, often renders him more idle and more worthless, and thus induces the real or supposed necessity of still greater harshness, on the part of the master. Such is the tendency of that comparison which the slave cannot easily avoid making, between his own situation and that of the free people of his own colour, who are his companions, and in every thing, except exemption from the authority of a master, his equals: whose condition, though often much worse than his own, naturally appears better to him; and being continually under his observation, and in close contact with his feelings, is apt to chafe goad and irritate him incessantly. This effect indeed is not always produced, but such is the tendency of this state of things; and it operates more extensively, and with greater force, than is commonly supposed.

But this effect, injurious as it must be to the character and conduct of the slaves, and consequently to their comfort and happiness, is far from being the worst that is produced by the existence of free blacks among us. A vast majority of the free blacks, as we have seen, are and must be an idle worthless and thievish race. It is with this part of them that the slaves will necessarily associate the most frequently, and the most intimately. Free blacks of the better class, who gain a comfortable subsistence by regular industry, keep as much as possible aloof from the slaves, to whom in general they regard themselves as in some degree superior. Their association is confined, as much as possible, to the better and more respectable class of slaves. But the idle and disorderly free blacks naturally seek the society of such slaves as are disposed to be idle and disorderly too, whom they encourage to be more and more so, by their example, their conversation, and the shelter and means of concealment which they furnish. They encourage the slaves to theft, because they partake in its fruits. They receive secrete and dispose of the stolen goods; a part, and probably much the larger part, of which they often receive as a reward for their services. They furnish places of meeting and hiding places in their houses, for the idle and the vicious slaves, whose idleness and vice are thus increased and rendered more contagious. These hiding places and places of meeting are so many traps and snares for the young and thoughtless slaves, who have not yet become vicious: so many schools in which they are taught, by precept and example, idleness lying debauchery drunkenness and theft. The consequence of all this is very easily seen, and I am sure is severely felt in all places, where free people of colour exist in considerable numbers. That so many resist this contagion; that the free blacks themselves, as well as the slaves, do not become still more profligate, is a strong and consoling proof that the race possesses a fund of good dispositions, and is capable, in a proper situation and under proper management, of becoming a virtuous and happy people. To place them in such a situation, to give them the benefit of such management, is the object of your noble enterprize, and surely no object is more entitled to approbation.

Great, however, as the benefits are which we may thus promise ourselves, from the colonization of the free people of colour, by its tendency to prevent the discontent and corruption of our slaves, and to secure to them a better treatment by rendering them more worthy of it, there is another advantage infinitely greater, in every point of view, to which it may lead the way. It tends, and may powerfully tend, to rid us gradually and entirely in the United States, of slaves and slavery: a great moral and political evil, of increasing virulence and extent, from which much mischief is now felt, and very great calamity in future is justly apprehended. It is in this point of view, I confess, that your scheme of colonization most strongly recommends itself, in my opinion, to attention and support. The alarming danger of cherishing in our bosom a distinct nation, which can never become incorporated with us, while it rapidly increases in numbers, and improves in intelligence; learning from us the arts of peace and war, the secret of its own strength, and the talent of combining and directing its force: a nation which must ever be hostile to us, from feeling and interest, because it can never incorporate with us, nor participate in the advantages which we enjoy: the danger of such a nation in our bosom need not be pointed out, to any reflecting mind. It speaks not only to our understandings, but to our very senses: and, however it may be derided by some, or overlooked by others, who have not the ability or the leisure, or do not give themselves the trouble, to reflect on and estimate properly the force and extent of those great moral and physical causes, which prepare gradually and at length bring forth the most terrible convulsions in civil society; it will not be viewed without deep and awful apprehension, by any who shall bring sound minds, and some share of political knowledge and sagacity, to the serious consideration of the subject. Such persons will give their most serious attention to any proposition, which has for its object the eradication of this terrible mischief, lurking in our vitals. I shall presently have occasion to advert a little to the manner in which your intended colony will conduce to this great end. It is, therefore, unnecessary to touch on it here. Indeed it is too obvious to require much explanation.

But independently of this view of the case, there is enough in the proposed measure to command our attention and support, on the score of benefit to ourselves.

No person who has seen the slave holding states, and those where slavery does not exist, and has compared ever so slightly their condition and situation, can have failed to be struck with the vast difference in favour of the latter. This difference extends to every thing, except only the character and manners of the most opulent and best educated people. These are very much the same every where. But in population; in the general diffusion of wealth and comfort; in public and private improvements; in the education manners and mode of life, among the middle and labouring classes; in the face of the country; in roads bridges and inns; in schools and churches; in the general advancement of improvement and prosperity there is no comparison. The change is seen the instant you cross the line, which separates the country where there are slaves, from that where there are none. Even in the same state, the parts where slaves most abound are uniformly the worst cultivated, the poorest, and the least populous; while wealth and improvement uniformly increase, as the number of slaves in the country diminishes. I might prove and illustrate this position by many examples, drawn from a comparison of different states, as Maryland and Pennsylvania, and between different counties in the same state, as Charles county and Frederick in Maryland; but it is unnecessary, because everybody who has seen the different parts of the country has been struck by this difference.

Whence does it arise? I answer from this, that in one division of the country the land is cultivated by freemen, for their own benefit; and in the other almost entirely by slaves, for the benefit of their masters. It is the obvious interest of the first class of labourers, to produce as much and consume as little as possible; and of the second class to consume as much and produce as little as possible. What the slave consumes is for himself: what he produces is for his master. All the time that he can withdraw from labour is gained to himself; all that he spends in labour is devoted to his master. All that the free labourer, on the contrary, can produce is for himself. All that he can save is so much added to his own stock. All the time that he loses from labour is his own loss.

This, if it were all, would probably be quite sufficient to account for the whole difference in question: but unfortunately it is far from being all. Another and a still more injurious effect of slavery remains to be considered.

Where the labouring class is composed wholly or in a very considerable degree of slaves, and of slaves distinguished from the free class by colour features and origin, the ideas of labour and of slavery soon become connected in the minds of the free class. This arises from that association of ideas, which forms one of the characteristic features of the human mind, and with which every reflecting person is well acquainted. They who continually from their infancy see black slaves employed in labour, and forming by much the most numerous class of labourers, insensibly associate the ideas of labour and of slavery, and are almost irresistibly led to consider labour as a badge of slavery, and consequently as a degradation. To be idle, on the contrary, is in their view the mark and the privilege of freemen. The effect of this habitual feeling upon the class of free whites who ought to labour, and consequently upon their condition, and the general condition of the country, will be readily perceived by those who reflect on such subjects. It is seen in the vast difference between the labouring class of whites in the southern and middle, and those of the northern and eastern states. Why are the latter incomparably more industrious, more thriving, more orderly, more comfortably situated than the former? The effect is obvious, to all those who have travelled through the different parts of our country. What is the cause? It is found in the association between the idea of slavery, and the idea of labour; and in the feeling produced by this association, that labour the proper occupation of negro slaves, and especially agricultural labour, is degrading to a free white man.

Thus we see that where slavery exists the slave labours as little as possible, because all the time that he can withdraw from labour is saved to his own enjoyments; and consumes as much as possible, because what he consumes belongs to his master: while the free white man is insensibly but irresistibly led, to regard labour the occupation of slaves as a degradation, and to avoid it as much as he can. The effect of these combined and powerful causes, steadily and constantly operating in the same direction, may easily be conceived. It is seen in the striking difference which exists, between the slave holding sections of our country, and those where slavery is not permitted.

It is therefore obvious, that a vast benefit would be conferred on the country, and especially on the slave holding districts, if all the slave labourers could be gradually and imperceptibly withdrawn from cultivation, and their place supplied by free white labourers. I say gradually and imperceptibly; because if it were possible to withdraw suddenly and at once, so great a portion of the effective labour of the community as is now supplied by slaves, it would be productive of the most disastrous consequences. It would create an immense void, which could not be filled. It would impoverish a great part of the community, unhinge the whole frame of society in a large portion of the country, and probably end in the most destructive convulsions. But it is clearly impossible, and therefore we need not enlarge on the evils which it would produce.

But to accomplish this great and beneficial change, gradually and imperceptibly; to substitute a free white class of cultivators for the slaves, with the consent of the owners, by a slow but steady and certain operation; I hold to be as practicable as it would be beneficial; and I regard this scheme of colonization as the first step in that great enterprize.

The considerations stated in the first part of this letter, have long since produced a thorough conviction in my mind, that the existence of a class of free people of colour in this country is highly injurious, to the whites the slaves and the free people of colour themselves: consequently that all emancipation, to however small an extent, which permits the persons emancipated to remain in this country, is an evil, which must increase with the increase of the operation, and would become altogether intolerable, if extended to the whole, or even to a very large part, of the black population. I am, therefore, strongly opposed to emancipation, in every shape and degree, unless accompanied by colonization.

I may perhaps on some future occasion develope a plan, on which I have long meditated, for colonizing gradually and with the consent of their owners, and of themselves where free, the whole coloured population, slaves and all: but this is not the proper place for such an explanation, for which indeed I have not time now. But it is an essential part of the plan, and of every such plan, to prepare the way for its adoption and execution, by commencing a colony of blacks, in a suitable situation and under proper management. This is what your society propose to accomplish. Their project, therefore, if rightly formed and well conducted, will open the way for this more extensive and beneficial plan, of removing gradually and imperceptibly, but certainly, the whole coloured population from the country, and leaving its place to be imperceptibly supplied, as it would necessarily be, by a class of free white cultivators. In every part of the country this operation must necessarily be slow. In the southern and southwestern states it will be very long before it can be accomplished, and a very considerable time must probably elapse, before it can even commence. It will begin first, and be first completed, in the middle states; where the evils of slavery are most sensibly felt, the desire of getting rid of the slaves is already strong, and a greater facility exists of supplying their place, by white cultivators. From thence it will gradually extend to the south and south west; till by its steady constant and imperceptible operation the evils of slavery shall be rooted out, from every part of the United States, and the slaves themselves and their posterity shall be converted into a free civilized and great nation, in the country from which their progenitors were dragged, to be wretched themselves and a curse to the whites.

This great end is to be attained in no other way, than by a plan of universal colonization, founded on the consent of the slave holders, and of the colonists themselves. For such a plan that of the present colonization society opens and prepares the way, by exploring the ground, selecting a proper situation, and planting a colony, which may serve as a receptacle a nursery and a school for those that are to follow. It is in this point of view that I consider its benefits as the most extensive and important, though not the most immediate.

The advantages of this undertaking to which I have hitherto adverted, are confined to ourselves. They consist in ridding us of the free people of colour, and preparing the way for getting rid of the slaves and of slavery. In these points of view they are undoubtedly very great. But there are advantages to the free blacks themselves, to the slaves, and to the immense population of middle and southern Africa, which no less recommend this undertaking, to our cordial and zealous support.

To the free blacks themselves the benefits are the most obvious, and will be the most immediate. Here they are condemned to a state of hopeless inferiority, and consequent degradation. As they cannot emerge form this state, they lose by degrees the hope and at last the desire of emerging. With this hope and desire they lose the most powerful incitements to industry, frugality, good conduct, and honourable exertion. For want of this incitement, this noble and ennobling emulation, they sink for the most part into a state of sloth wretchedness and profligacy. The few honourable exceptions serve merely to show of what the race is capable, in a proper situation. Transplanted to a colony composed of themselves alone, they would enjoy real equality: in other words real freedom. They would become proprietors of land, master mechanics, ship owners, navigators and merchants, and by degrees schoolmasters, justices of the peace, militia officers, ministers of religion, judges, and legislators. There would be no white population to remind them of, and to perpetuate, their original inferiority; but enjoying all the privileges of freedom, they would soon enjoy all its advantages, and all its dignity. The whites who might visit them, would visit them as equals; for the purposes of a commerce mutually advantageous. They would soon feel the noble emulation to excel, which is the fruitful source of excellence, in all the various departments of life; and under the influence of this generous and powerful sentiment, united with the desire and hope of improving their condition, the most universal and active incitements to exertion among men, they would rise rapidly in the scale of existence, and soon become equal to the people of Europe or of European origin, so long their masters and oppressors. Of all this the most intelligent among them would soon become sensible. The others would learn it from them; and the prospect and hope of such blessings would have an immediate and most beneficial effect, on their condition and character. For it will be easy to adopt such regulations, as to exclude from this colony all but those who shall deserve, by their conduct to be admitted: thus rendering the hope of admission a powerful incentive, to industry honesty and religion.

To the slaves the advantages, though not so obvious or immediate, are yet certain and great.

In the first place they would be greatly benefited by the removal of the free blacks, who now corrupt them, and render them discontented: thus exposing them to harsher treatment, and greater privations. In the next place, this measure will open the way to their more frequent and easier manumission: for many persons who are now restrained from manumitting their slaves, by the conviction that they generally become a nuisance when manumitted in the country, would gladly give them freedom, if they were to be sent to a place where they might enjoy it, usefully to themselves and to society. And lastly, as this species of manumission, attended by removal to a country where they might obtain all the advantages of freedom, would be a great blessing, and would soon be so considered by the slaves, the hope of deserving and obtaining it would be a great solace to their sufferings, and a powerful incitement to good conduct. It would thus tend to make them happier and better before it came, and to fit them better for usefulness and happiness afterwards.

Such a colony, too, would enlarge the range of civilization and commerce, and thus tend to the benefit of all civilized and commercial nations. In this benefit our own nation would most largely participate: because we having founded the colony, and giving it constant supplies of new members, as well as its first and principal supply of necessaries and comforts, its first connexions would be formed with us, and would naturally grow with its growth and our own, till they ripened into fixed habits of intercourse friendship and attachment.

The greatest benefit, however, to be hoped from this enterprize, that which in contemplation most delights the philanthropic mind, still remains to be unfolded. It is the benefit to Africa herself, from this return of her children to her bosom, bearing with them arts knowledge and civilization, to which she has hitherto been a stranger. Cast your eyes my dear sir on this vast continent. Pass over the northern and north eastern parts, and the great desert, where sterility ferocious ignorance and fanaticism seem to hold exclusive and perpetual sway. Fix your attention on Soudan, and the widely extended regions to the south. You see there innumerable tribes and nations of blacks, mild and humane in their disposition, sufficiently intelligent, robust active and vigorous, not averse from labour or wholly ignorant of agriculture, and possessing some knowledge of the ruder arts, which minister to the first wants of civilized man. You see a soil generally fertile, a climate healthy for the natives, and a mighty river, which rolls its waters through vast regions inhabited by these tribes, and seems destined by an all wise and beneficent Providence, one day to connect them with each other, and all of them with the rest of the world, in the relations of commerce and friendly intercourse. What a field is here presented for the blessings of civilization and Christianity, which colonies of civilized blacks afford the best and probably the only means of introducing? These colonies, composed of blacks already instructed in the arts of civilized life and the truths of the gospel, judiciously placed well conducted and constantly enlarged, will extend gradually into the interior, will form commercial and political connexions with the native tribes in their vicinity, will extend those connexions to tribes more and more remote, will incorporate many of the natives with the colonies, and in their turn make establishments and settlements among the natives, and thus diffuse all around the arts of civilization, and the benefits of literary moral and religious instruction.

That such must be the tendency of colonies of this discription, if well placed well formed and well conducted, cannot I think be reasonably doubted. Such a colony has already been established, with satisfactory success, and flattering prospects. But it may be doubted perhaps whether the situation has been fortunately chosen, with respect to all the objects that ought to be kept in view; and it is still more questionable whether a sufficient supply of colonists, of a proper description, to give it the extent necessary for rendering it in any considerable degree beneficial, can be drawn from the sources on which it must rely. It is in the United States alone that such colonists can be found, in any considerable numbers. In the choice of a good situation too, on which so much depends, we have far more assistance from recent discoveries, and the extension of geographical knowledge in that quarter of the globe, than was possessed by the founders of that colony. We have the benefit of their experience, of their discoveries, and even of their errors; which we may be able to correct or avoid. Useful therefore and meritorious as their establishment certainly is, we may hope to render ours far more extensively beneficial.

An objection of some plausibility is frequently urged, against this scheme of colonizing the free people of colour, which it may be proper in this place to notice. These people it is said, especially the industrious and estimable part of them, will not go to the new colony. That many of them will decline to go at first, and some always, cannot be doubted. It is even probable, and may be safely admitted, that but few of them now think favourably of the project: for men, especially ignorant men, venture unwillingly upon great changes, the extent nature and consequences of which they are little capable of understanding. But it by no means follows that the same unwillingness or hesitation will continue, after the ground shall have been broken, the way opened, and a settlement formed. In the first instance none will engage, but the most industrious intelligent and enterprising, who are capable of discerning the advantages of the undertaking, and have resolution and energy enough to encounter its first hardships and risks. This is the case with all colonies, and especially those formed in distant unknown or unsettled countries. Some resolute and adventurous spirits first embark; and they open and prepare the way for others. It is stated and believed, on evidence better known to you than to me, that a sufficient number of such persons stand ready at this time to commence the colony, as soon as the necessary previous arrangements can be made. I have no doubt of the fact, not only from information, but from general reasoning on the human character, and my knowledge of many individuals among the free blacks. When this first step is taken, and in most enterprises the great difficulty lies in the first step; when a settlement of free blacks shall have actually been formed, the way opened, and the first difficulties surmounted; others will soon be disposed to follow. If successful and prosperous, as it certainly will be if properly conducted, its success will quickly become known to the free blacks, in every part of the country.

However distrustful of the whites, they will confide in the reports made to them by people of their own colour and class. The prosperity of the settlement, and the advantageous condition of the settlers, will soon be universally understood and believed; and indeed will be far more apt to be exaggerated than undervalued. The most ignorant and stupid of the free people of colour will speedily understand, or believe, that in the colony they may obtain a state of equality opulence and distinction, to which they can never aspire in this country. Hence the desire to join their friends and equals there, may be expected soon to become general among them: nor is it too much to hope and anticipate, that this desire will speedily grow into a passion; that the difficulty will be not to find colonists, but to select them; and that the hope of being received into the favoured number, for whom it may be practicable to provide annually, will ere long become a most powerful and operative incentive, to industry sobriety and general good conduct, among the whole class from which the selection will be annually made.

Having detained your thus long, my dear sir, much too long I am afraid, with these preliminary observations on the benefits which may be expected from this undertaking, I proceed now to the manner of carrying it into execution. I shall not however treat this branch of the subject in its whole extent, for which this is not the proper place; but shall confine myself to the objects more immediately in view at this time; the choice of a proper situation for the first settlement, and the circumstances to which the attention of the agent who is to be sent out for the purpose of exploring the ground, ought chiefly to be directed.

The first of these circumstances is salubrity; with a view to which the vicinity of low and marshy grounds, of swamps, and of rivers which are apt to overflow their banks, ought to be carefully avoided. High situations, open to the sea, or washed by rivers with high and steep banks, should be sought. Mountains in the vicinity, and in the direction from which the winds regularly blow, are much to be desired; and great attention should be paid to the abundance of brooks and springs, and to the quality of their water. On all these accounts an elevated and uneven surface ought to be preferred, though less fertile than the flat low grounds. Too much attention ought not to be paid, in the first settlements, either to great fertility or the convenience of navigation. The first establishment should no doubt be within a convenient distance from a good port, but need not be close to it; nor ought to be so, unless the immediate vicinity should be much more healthy, than such situations usually are. The settlement must be entirely agricultural at first, and will long perhaps always continue so, in a very great degree. Commerce there, as in our own country, must and will soon grow out of agriculture; but the first settlements ought to be made with a view to the latter, far more than to the former. Cintiguity to a good market for agricultural productions, is indeed a very important excitement and aid to agricultural industry, and therefore a very important circumstance in the location of an agricultural colony; but it is far from being the most important, and care must be taken to prevent its being too much regarded.

Nor ought any thing in this respect to be sacrificed to great fertility; which is most frequently found in low flat and unwholesome situations. A good soil, well adapted to the cultivation of wheat, Indian corn or maize, and cotton, is all in this respect that ought to be desired: and such soils are found in places possessing every advantage of good water, with a dry and pure atmosphere. Wheat and Indian corn are the best articles of food, and the soils that produce them are fit also for various other grains and vegetables, useful for food and of easy culture; especially the sweet potato and various kinds of pulse, which thrive well in hot climates. As an object of tillage, with a view to exportation, cotton is by far the best, because it thrives well in high and healthy situations, of a light soil, may be cultivated to advantage on small farms, and requires little labour which cannot be performed by women and children.

Attention should also be paid to suitable streams, for the erection of grist mills saw mills and other water works, which will be almost indispensable to the colony in its infant state, and of great utility at a more advanced period. Fortunately such streams abound most, in the countries best adapted in other respects to agricultural settlements.

The character condition and disposition of the natives will also require very particular attention; it being of the greatest importance to gain and preserve their good will, so as to cultivate and cement a free and friendly intercourse with them, to obtain from them assistance and supplies, and gradually to communicate to them the knowledge and habits of civilized life. For this essential purpose, we should not only avoid the neighbourhood of fierce and warlike tribes, but that of very large and powerful ones; who will be much more unmanageable and dangerous than small ones, in many points of view.

It would also be best to select a situation as distant as possible from Sierra Leone. There would no doubt be some advantages, at first, in a close neighborhood; but they would probably soon be overbalanced, by the jealousies and collisions which could hardly fail to take place, between two colonies established under different governments, and with different views and interests in many important points. This is an objection to Sherborough river; probably not insurmountable, but sufficient to turn the scale in favour of a more distant position, possessing in other respects equal or nearly equal advantages.

If indeed an arrangement could be made with the British government, for an union and incorporation of the two colonies, or rather for the reception of our colonists into their settlements, it might deserve serious consideration. There would no doubt be many advantages, at first, in sending them to a settlement already formed, where the first difficulties have been surmounted, and a regular government exists. But this is matter for future deliberation. We ought now to search out a fit place for ourselves; for it is doubtful whether an incorporation would be agreed to by the British government, and far from being certain that the best place has been chosen for their establishment. When these points shall have been ascertained, and we know what prospect there is of obtaining a suitable situation elsewhere, a negociation may be opened, if then thought adviseable, for uniting the two colonies.

There will always be one strong objection to this incorporation. The British colony will be a long time retained in the colonial state, subject to a foreign and distant government; and when ripe for independence, will probably be compelled to seek it by force of arms. The nature and habitual policy of that government will almost necessarily lead to this result. Our colony, on the contrary, ought to be republican from the beginning, and formed and fashioned with a view to self–government and independence, with the consent of the mother country, at the earliest practicable period. It is thus only that it can be most useful to the colonists, to Africa, to us, and to the general cause of humanity.

It would, however, be premature at present, to decide on the question of incorporation; and therefore with a view to this interesting part of the case, the agent should be instructed to investigate most carefully the progress and present state of the Sierra Leone settlement, and to ascertain as exactly as possible all the circumstances of its locality, as relates to health, objects of culture suitable to its soil and climate, navigation, the nature of the country in its vicinity, the character situation and strength of the neighbouring tribes, and the facilities of communication with the remote and interior parts of the continent.

One very important circumstance, in the selection of a suitable place for our settlements, to which the attention of the agent ought to be particularly directed, still remains to be brought into view. I mean the facility of communication with the Niger, that mighty river, which seems destined to supply the link of connexion, between the interior of Africa and the civilized world.

I take the question relative to the lower course and termination of the Niger to be now satisfactorily settled. The discoveries of Park in his last journey, compared and connected with the information derived from Mr Maxwell and others, concerning the river Zayr, improperly called the Congo, from the name of a little district at its mouth, to say nothing of Sidi Hamet's narrative as given to us by Captain Riley, which deserves great attention, authorize us I think to conclude that these two rivers are the same: in other words that the Niger, after having traversed the interior of Africa four thousand miles, falls under the name of the Zayr into the Atlantic, south of the equator: thus laying open that vast continent to its inmost recesses, and bringing its immense population into contact with the rest of the world. There is some doubt and much contrariety of opinion in this point, and this is not the place for entering at large into the discussion. Fortunately a decision of the question, which cannot be absolutely decided till the course of the Niger shall be pursued to its termination, is not necessary for our present purpose: for whether this great body of waters, collected in a course of two thousand miles, be lost, according to the opinion of some, in the sands marshes and lakes supposed to exist in the centre of Africa; or, as others have imagined, be discharged into the Mediterranean through the Nile, a river of a more elevated bed, and hardly a tenth part as large; or being arrested in its progress eastward, toward the Indian ocean, by the elevated country in which the western Nile has its sources, is driven through the feebler barrier of the mountains on the south, and thrown off to the southern Atlantic; it is still the only avenue into the interior of Africa: and a noble avenue it is. At Bammakoo, where Park struck it in his last journey, he states it to be a mile wide. From thence to Houssa, a distance of between six and seven hundred miles, its course has been satisfactorily ascertained. Throughout this great extent, in which it receives many large streams, and flows through a fertile country, its current though strong is smooth and even, uninterrupted by cateracts and shoals. As it advances eastward it recedes more and more from the coast, and thus becomes more and more difficult of access. Settlements therefore on the Atlantic, formed with a view to commercial intercourse with the vast countries on the Niger, and those more distant to which it leads, must be placed as near as possible to its upper waters, where they first begin to be navigable for boats.

These waters probably approach much nearer the Atlantic, than has hitherto been believed. We have seen that at Bammakoo, the highest point to which the Niger has yet been traced, it is a mile wide: as large as the Susquehanna at its entrance into the Chesapeake bay. It must therefore be a very considerable stream, much higher up: that is much further to the southwest, and consequently much nearer to the Atlantic. It has its source in the western part of a chain of mountains, which runs from west to east, nearly parallel with that part of the coast of Africa, which extends from Sierra Leone to the Bite of Benin.—These mountains separate it from the rivers, which, rising on their southern side, fall into the Atlantic, in the neighbourhood of Sierra Leone. Their sources no doubt approach very near to those of the Niger. Probably no great distance divides its navigable waters from theirs. Such a river, with a good port at or near its mouth, and a fertile country on its banks, would present the proper situation for a colony, planted with a view to the civilization of Africa, by the commerce of the Niger.

The course of such a commerce would be, to ascend the Atlantic river as far as possible in boats, with the commodities wanted for the interior consumption; and to establish at that point a place of deposit, from whence the merchandize would be sent over land to the Niger, and down it to the various markets below. The returns would go up the Niger to its highest navigable point, where a town would soon arise. From thence they would pass by land, to the place of deposit on the other side of the mountain; and there be put into boats, for transportation down the river to the shipping port. If the Niger should be ascertained to continue its course to the ocean, an intercourse would gradually be extended down to its mouth, where a great commercial city would arise; and to this mart the return cargoes purchased above would gradually find their way, down the stream. Thus an immense circle of commerce would imperceptibly be formed, embracing the whole course of the Niger, and the vast countries which it waters and lays open, and connecting them all with each other, and with the whole commercial world. For a very considerable time this commerce would be confined to the countries far up the river, near to its source; where settlements would first be formed, and civilization would commence. As the communication between these first settlements and those on the Atlantic became more and more safe easy and expeditious, by means of intermediate settlements good roads and improved inland navigation, colonies and trade would extend further and further down the river. Other settlements would soon be commenced at its mouth. At last these two branches would meet and unite, in a commerce vast as the stream on which it would be borne, and as the continent which it would civilize enlighten and adorn.

Ages indeed may be required, for the full attainment of these objects. Untoward events or unforeseen difficulties may retard or defeat them. But the prospect, however remote or uncertain, is still animating, and the hope of success seems sufficient to stimulate us to the utmost exertion. How vast and sublime a career does this undertaking open to a generous ambition, aspiring to deathless fame by great and useful actions! Who can count the millions, that in future times shall know and bless the names of those, by whom this magnificent scheme of beneficence and philantrophy has been conceived, and shall be carried into execution? Throughout the widely extended regions of middle and southern Africa, then filled with populous and polished nations, their memories shall be cherished and their praises sung; when other states, and even the flourishing and vigorous nation to which they belong, now in its flower of youth, shall have run their round of rise grandeur and decay, and like the founders of Palmyra Tyre Babylon Memphis and Thebes, shall no longer be known, except by vague reports of their former greatness, or by some fragments of those works of art, the monuments of their taste their power or their pride, which they may leave behind.

It is in connection, my dear sir, with this great operation, that I consider your proposed colony of free blacks as most interesting and important. It ought to be the first step in this splendid career, and to be located with that view. In choosing a situation for it, therefore, the greatest regard ought to be had to its future connection with the Niger. To this end the agent ought to be instructed, to make the most careful enquiries concerning the sources of that river, and its highest or most southwestern point. He should also make every effort to obtain the most full and accurate information, concerning the rivers that rise on the opposite side of the mountains, and take their course southwestwardly to the ocean. Their size, the nature of the country through which they flow, the height to which they are navigable for ships and for boats, and the harbours at or near their mouths, should all be ascertained with the utmost care and accuracy. That river which combines in the greatest degree, the advantages of salubrity soil navigation and good neighbourhood, and at the same time brings us nearest to the navigable waters of the Niger, by a good pass over the intervening mountains, is, I apprehend, the proper place, in itself, for the establishment of our colony.

I say in itself: because a place combining all those advantages may still be very unfit for our purpose, if it lie within the claims of any European power, or too near any of their settlements. It should therefore be a particular object of the agent's attention, to ascertain the situation and extent of those claims, and the distance between any European settlements and such place as may appear suited to our views. Enquiries concerning the territorial claims of European powers can best be made in London; but it is in Africa alone that such information, when obtained, can be applied to the object of the intended mission.

There is a river called in some maps the Mesurada, which, as there laid down, extends its branches further northeast than any other, and enters the ocean about one hundred or one hundred and fifty miles southeast of the Sherborough. It deserves I think the particular attention of the agent, who should be instructed to make enquiries about it, with a view to all the circumstances which may render it proper for a settlement, and to visit it, should the result of this investigation offer encouragement.

The river Nunez or Noones also merits particular regard. It empties itself into the Atlantic in latitude 10° 1' north, about one hundred and fifty miles northwest from Sierra Leone. It has a very good harbour at its mouth, and carries from six to eight fathom of water about twenty miles up, to a bar, over which there is however three fathom, or eighteen feet. After passing the bar the water continues from five to eight fathom deep, to a point about fifty miles up from the mouth. From thence to the falls about fifty miles higher up, it is said to admit vessels of one hundred and twenty tons. The country around and above the falls is represented as elevated fertile and healthy; abounding in game, well supplied with excellent timber, and watered by numerous streams large enough for mills. Indian corn, and all sorts of pulse and garden vegetables, are said to grow luxuriantly. Cattle abound so much, than an ox is sold for a dollar. The country below yields rice, Indian corn, and all the usual tropical productions. The natives are represented as peaceable and friendly, and the principal chief, who resides about ninety miles up the river, a little below the falls, and whose authority extends down to the mouth, and far into the interior, is said to be a man of sense and abilities, of a mild and humane character, and favourably disposed towards the whites, especially the Americans. He speaks English perfectly well. This place would seem therefore to deserve the particular attention of the agent and the society. In addition to its other advantages its upper waters approach near to the river Grande; a very important and interesting feature of African geography, as respects commercial intercourse with the interior, and the extension of civilization by means of colonies of civilized blacks.

These, my dear sir, are the hints that I thought I might venture to suggest to you, on this most interesting subject. I make no apology for the length of my letter. It might no doubt be curtailed with advantage. But it might also, and with more ease, if not to a better purpose, be very much enlarged: for I have touched briefly on less important topics, and altogether omitted some which belong properly to the subject, but did not seem to require immediate attention. Such as it is I submit it to your consideration, with the hope that it may be of some use, in the preparatory arrangements which you are engaged in making.

With the best wishes I am
Dear Sir,
Your most obedient servant,
ROB. G. HARPER

ELIAS B. CALDWELL, ESQ.
Secretary of the Colonization
Society of the United States

C.

Speech on the Missouri Question[*]

————·••··————

I WILL NOW SIR, consider a little the cases of Kentucky and Tennessee, which came into the Union before Ohio, but in a different manner, and did not go so far back for the origin of the conditions on which they became states. The first was formed out of the state of Virginia; and was in fact the first new state received in to the Union: for Vermont, although admitted before it, could not for the reasons already mentioned, be correctly regarded as a new state. The act of Assembly of Virginia, for erecting Kentucky into a state, was passed on the 18th of December, 1789. It imposes restrictions on the new state, limiting the exercise of its legislative powers, in several important points. The lands of non residents were not to be taxed higher than those of resident proprietors. This is a very important legislative power, very freely exercised by some of the old states, and possessed by all. But it was withheld from Kentucky. Again: she was to make no grants of land or issue any land warrants, for about two years, which might interfere with land warrants previously issued by Virginia. This was a just and proper restriction; but still it was a restriction on the sovereign power of granting vacant land, and a restriction too of an extensive effect, on account of the peculiar nature of Virginia land warrants, commonly called treasury warrants, which were not confined to any designated spot or tract of land, but might be located any where within the whole country open to warrants, where a sufficient quantity of vacant land could be found. The effect of the restriction consequently was, that Kentucky should make no grants of vacant land for nearly two years. It was also declared, that the navigation of the Ohio, so far as it touched the territory of the new state, should be free and common to the citizens of the United States. That is, no tolls should be levied by the new

---

[*] Delivered in the Maryland Senate on 19 January 1820 and later published in the *Federal Gazette and Baltimore Daily Advertiser*, 7-10 February 1820. This newspaper has never been microfilmed. One of two extant copies can be found at the main branch of the Enoch Pratt Free Library in Baltimore. See also *Niles' Register*, 19 February 1820. Obvious typographical errors have been corrected, though the idiosyncracies of Harper's syntax and spelling remain unchanged.

state, on the navigation of the Ohio. The right of levying tolls is a clear attribute of sovereignty, and generally considered as a very important one. It was withdrawn from Kentucky by this compact. There were other restrictions imposed on her, but these are the most important. Did Kentucky because of these restrictions, not existing in the other states under the federal constitution, ever regard herself as inferior to the other states? Will she admit, or will any one contend, that she is not at this moment and at all times a *state*, within the meaning of the terms as used in the constitution? There are some points indeed, and material ones too, in which *they* can legislate and *she* cannot; but the difference was produced by compact, with her own consent, and therefore it does not impair or affect her character of sovereignty. She gave this consent indeed to the state of Virginia, with which the compact was made, and not to the United States; but that can make no difference in the principle. They are still restrictions, though imposed or more properly speaking, required by Virginia, instead of the United States. Virginia in treating on this subject with the people of Kentucky, acted as a distinct community or sovereignty. They did so too; and the transaction, like those by which new states are received into the Union, was strictly speaking a compact. When the state was afterwards admitted into the Union, no conditions were required, because all that were deemed important had been already stipulated by Virginia, or were precluded by the compact formed between her and the United States, by her act of cession and their acceptance.

The case of Tennessee, Mr. President, resembles that of Kentucky, in some points of view. Tennessee, it will be remembered, was originally a part of North Carolina, which state, in December 1789, ceded it to the United States. Various conditions were annexed to the cession, one of which necessarily extended, and no doubt was meant to extend, to the new state which the act of cession required congress to erect in the ceded territory. This condition was "that the lands of non-residents should not be taxed higher than those of residents." When congress, by the act of June 1st, 1796, admitted this territory, as the state of Tennessee, into the Union, no new conditions were required; but this respecting the lands of non-residents remained in operation, and restricted in this particular case the sovereignty and legislative power of the new state. Nevertheless it has always regarded itself, and been viewed by the rest of the Union, as a "state", within the constitutional meaning of that term.

Three others have since been admitted, besides Indiana and Illinois.

The first of them was Louisiana. Her case will be found very strongly to illustrate and exemplify the principle for which I contend. The principle, I will here repeat, is, that "conditions required of a state on its admission, limiting and restraining the exercise of its legislative powers in certain defined cases, and assented to by it, are not inconsistent with its character as a *state*, within the meaning of the constitution, and are therefore not repugnant to the constitution." It will soon appear how strongly this principle is supported by the case of Louisiana.

That state was admitted under the act of April 8th, 1812. Numerous and very important conditions were required. This new state was to relinquish all claim to the vacant lands. No lands sold by the United States were to be taxed until five years after the sales. Lands of non-residents were not to be taxed higher than those of residents. The rivers were to be free—that is, free from tolls for transportation on them. The state constitution was to be consistent with the principles of civil and religious liberty. The trial by jury was to be maintained in criminal cases. The writ of habeas corpus was to be allowed, and finally the records and legislative acts, and the judicial proceedings, were to be kept in the English language, which, it is well known, was not the language of the country. These, no doubt, were very proper restrictions—but they were restrictions on the legislative powers of the new state, not known to the original states, or the federal constitution. But Louisiana consented to them, as the price of her admission into the Union. Is she, therefore, not a "state" within the meaning of the constitution? She certainly thinks herself so, and has been considered so by every body else. And why? Because conditions proposed to her and accepted by her, altho' they restrain the exercise of her sovereign power in certain defined, tho' very important cases, are to be regarded as restrictions imposed by herself; and, consequently, as consistent with the character of sovereignty.

I will now ask your attention Mr. President, to the case of Mississippi. That state was originally a part of Georgia and was ceded to the United Sates in April 1802. The act of cession required, that "the conditions and restrictions of the ordinance of July 13th, 1787, should be extended to the ceded territory; that article only excepted which forbids slavery." On the 1st of March, 1817, Congress passed an act, under which the western part of this territory was admitted into the Union, as the State of Mississippi. That act required as a condition of the admittance, that the ordinance should be maintained by the new state, except so far as related to the prohibition of slavery. It has been seen, sir, how many restrictions on legislative power, beyond those imposed by the federal constitution on the original states, this ordinance contains; all of them, one only excepted, were required of this new state, as conditions of its reception into the Union. Such of them as were deemed most important were repeated, and specially required: such as, that lands sold by the United States should remain untaxed five years from the sale; that lands of non–residents should not be taxed higher than those of residents; that the lands of the United Sates should never be taxed, and that the rivers should be free. The new state assented to them all. Alabama the youngest daughter of this great and flourishing family of republics, did the same thing. She came in by the act of March 2d. 1819. The same conditions were required of her, and she assented, to them all. These conditions, indeed, did not restrain the admission of slaves; but they did restrain the exercise of other legislative powers, standing precisely on the same footing of sovereignty; and yet these states like the rest are deemed sovereign. They are considered as "States" with in the meaning of the constitution. Nay more, they and all the others are expressly declared in the several acts for their admission, to be admitted into the Union, "on an equal footing with the original states."

After these numerous examples, this long course of practice, it might reasonably have been expected, sir, that the constitutional question would be considered as settled. I think the position strong on the constitution itself and fortified as it is by this long and uniform usage, I must consider it as impregnable. I will now proceed to the next objection, which applies exclusively to the countries west of the Mississippi, and arises out of the treaty of April 30th, 1803 by which they were ceded to the United States. It is the 3d article that is supposed to create an obligation on the United States, to admit Mississippi as a state into the Union, without any condition restricting her from the introduction of slaves. The article runs thus:

"The inhabitants of the ceded territory shall be incorporated into the union of the United States, and admitted as soon as possible according to the principles of the federal constitution, to the enjoyment of all the rights, advantages, and immunities, of citizens of the United States: and in the meantime they shall be protected in the free enjoyment of their liberty, property, and the religion which they profess."

Some doubts may perhaps be entertained, about the extent and operation of this article. It may be viewed merely as a stipulation, that the people of the ceded countries shall be placed personally and individually on a footing, as to civil and political rights, with the people of the United States. If the first member of the clause stood alone, this, I should think, would be its true construction. But the second branch of it, "and in the meantime they shall be protected in the free enjoyment of their liberty, property, and the religion which they profess," shows, satisfactorily, that more was intended; and I concur in the opinion which has been declared in another place, by one of the most eminent statesmen of this or any other country, that this 3d article of the treaty of cession, though inaccurately and imperfectly expressed, must be understood to stipulate, in favor of the people of the ceded territory, that at a proper time, of which congress must, of course, be the judge, they shall be received as a state, or states, into the Union.

But this admission is to be "according to the principles of the federal constitution." This brings us back precisely to the same enquiry, in which we have already been engaged. "What are the principles of the federal constitution, in relation to the admission of new states into the Union? Do these principles imperatively require Congress to admit new states, whenever they may wish to come in, or under any given or defined circumstances? I have attempted to show that they do not, and I will not repeat the argument." Do they require that when new states are in a fit situation to come in, Congress shall be bound to receive them, without obtaining or asking any conditions whatever, to restrain them, with their own consent, in the exercise, in certain defined and specified cases, of any legislative power, possessed by the original states, however essential such restraints may be judged to the general welfare, with which Congress is specially charged by the constitution? I have endeavored to prove, with what success, it is not for me to judge, that nothing of this kind is required of Congress, by the principles of the federal constitution. That on the contrary, such conditions may be required, in conformity with those principles. Such I have attempted to show is the theory of the constitution, according to the soundest and clearest rules of construction. Such undoubtedly has been the uniform practice, in the admission of states formed out of our original territory. Are we called on to adopt a new and different rule, with respect to these recently acquired countries? Is it not a fulfillment of the treaty with respect to them, of this third article introduced for their benefit, if they are placed on an equal footing with the old territories, and admitted now at the eleventh hour, to an equal participation in all those benefits and privileges, which were originally gained through toil, danger, suffering and blood? Must they come in on different and more favorable terms, in order to be made equal, "according to the principles of the federal constitution?" I humbly conceive that such a claim cannot be supported. It is sufficient, if no other or greater conditions are required from them, greater in principle I mean, than have been required and obtained from other new states, formed out of our old territory. Some conditions required in other cases, it might be inexpedient to require in this. I think it inexpedient in this case, for reasons which I will presently state, to require the condition respecting slavery. But the right is denied, and that right, though its exercise is, in my opinion, inexpedient, in the present case, I consider as very important.

Thus, sir, I think the question as to Missouri will stand on general reasoning. But I consider it as having received a partial decision in the case of Louisiana. That state was embraced by the third article of the treaty of cession, equally with Missouri. It has been admitted under many conditions, abridging the exercise of its legislative powers, in many important cases. The power of admitting slaves from the other states and territories was not indeed restrained; but those that were restrained are equally legislative, and rest probably on the same principle. These powers I have already had occasion to enumerate, and they are in the recollection of the Senate. I have heard it contended or intimated, that either the constitution or the third article of the treaty of cession have been violated by those conditions required from Louisiana. That state has consented to them, and by its consent has gained admission into the Union. This practical commentary on the treaty and the constitution ought I conceive to settle its construction; even if the doubts on the subject were stronger in theory then they appear to me. Great is and ought to be the force of usage, in expounding laws and constitutions.

Before I leave this part of the subject sir, I will notice briefly an argument which has been urged by persons entitled to very high respect in support of the principle for which I contend. I will notice it, because in my opinion it is inadmissable, and I do not wish to be considered as concurring in it; as I might be, were I to pass it over in silence. This argument is founded on the use of the word "migration," in relation to slaves, in that part of the constitution which restrains Congress from prohibiting the importation of slaves before the year 1808. The provision is thus expressed: "The migration or importation of such persons as any of the states now existing shall think proper to admit, shall not be prohibited by Congress prior to the year 1808." This, it is said, is a restriction of the power to prohibit the introduction of slaves, which results from the general power to regulate commerce, and without this restriction would have taken effect immediately. As the power to regulate commerce extends to the commerce "among the several states," as well as to that "with foreign nations," it would, according to this argument, enable congress to prohibit the transfer of slaves from one state to another, as well as their introduction from abroad. Some of the states insisted on a suspension of this power for twenty years, as far as relates to slaves, and at their instance, this qualifying clause was introduced. The term "migration" was intended for the case of transfer from one state to another; and "importation" for that of introduction from foreign countries. If nothing but introduction from abroad had been in view, the term "importation" would have been sufficient; and the instrument, one of the most concise and accurate compositions in existence, shows that no words are used but such as are strictly appropriate, and necessary to convey the intended meaning. Consequently the use of the term "migration" proves, that something more than introduction from abroad is meant and it is strictly appropriate to the transfer of slaves from state to state. Therefore, it is to be inferred, that the power to prohibit such transfers, after the year 1807, is given to congress, as part of the general power to regulate commerce "among the several states." Such is the argument: certainly a very ingenious one, but, as I think, unsound. It seems to me to rest on a fallacy, and to prove too much, or too little. It certainly goes to invest congress with a very important and extensive power which that body has never, as far as I know, been heretofore supposed to possess; which it has never exercised or claimed; and to which, I believe, the states would not, and ought not, to have consented.

This argument assumes the position, that if nothing had been in view but the introduction of slaves from abroad, the word importation would have been sufficient, and "migration," consequently would not have been added. It is not I should think sound reasoning, or a very safe course, to infer a great constitutional power, from the mere use in the constitution of an additional word, which without the supposition of that power would be superfluous. But waiving this, I contend that the word "importation" would not cover the whole ground, of introduction from abroad. It applies solely to introduction by *sea*, for which it is the appropriate expression. But it must be recollected that slaves might have been then, or still may be, introduced by *land* from foreign countries. The whole of Louisiana, extending round our western and south western borders, was then a foreign country. Florida, bounding us to the south, was a foreign country. Those countries abounded with slaves, the introduction of which into the United States could not be correctly called an "importation." They would have been introduced by land. But Congress, under the general power to regulate commerce, would have been authorized to prohibit this introduction. This some of the southern states wished to prevent, for twenty years. They wished to keep open the introduction of slaves from abroad, either by land or water, till 1808. In this they were gratified, in order to gain their admission to the constitution; and to accomplish the object it was provided, that till 1808 Congress should not prohibit either the "migration" or "importation" of slaves. "Importation" applied to introduction by sea, and "migration" to introduction by land. Thus each of these terms has its distinct and proper effect, and the whole argument falls to the ground. It is also unsound because it proves too much, or too little. If it means that Congress may now, under the general power to regulate commerce among the several states, prohibit the owner of slaves in one state to remove with them and settle in another; or a person in one state who may acquire slaves in another, by marriage, bequest or distribution, to bring them home; the states into which they are in either case to be brought permitting their introduction; it will on that construction give a most novel and extraordinary effect to the power of regulating commerce, by extending it to operations with which commerce has no manner of connection. If on the other hand the agreement confines this prohibitory power to the case of purchasing slaves in one state for sale in another, it will fall entirely short of the intended object; which is the exclusion of slaves and slavery from the new states west of the Mississippi: for the owners of slaves may still, under this limited prohibition, emigrate with them to those countries.

I have bestowed this particular attention, sir, on this argument, because it has been advanced in quarters of high authority; and while I wish to defend and support the powers of the federal government, within their due limits, I am unwilling to see them enlarged, by what I consider as erroneous construction. I will now proceed to discuss that branch of the question which relates to the expediency of exercising, in this case, the power which I believe the general government to possess, of requiring conditions similar to this, from new states, on their introduction into the Union.

And here I fully concur in opinion with those who advocated the resolution in the other house. I think it inexpedient for congress to require this condition, in the case of Missouri. This opinion I have formed, contrary to my first impressions, after a very careful examination of the subject, and my reasons for it I will proceed to explain. I wish to explain them, not only to justify myself in the vote which I feel it my duty to give, but also in the hope that I may, perhaps, be fortunate enough to suggest something, tending to allay the apprehensions entertained, and, as I think, groundlessly entertained, on this subject, in many parts of the country.

These apprehensions appear to me to turn, in the first place, on the general increase of slavery in the United States, which, it is supposed, would result from leaving the state of Missouri at liberty to admit them. I think this fear unfounded, for several reasons. In the first place, Missouri, I feel confident, cannot long continue a slave holding state. It lies in the course of that immense and perennial stream of northern and eastern emigration, which flows over and fills Ohio, Indiana and Illinois, and has already passed the Mississippi. The southern and slave holding emigration cannot long resist this current. The eastern and northern emigrants are farmers, who require small tracts of land, and settle comfortably. The slave holders wish to be planters, and require larger tracts and sparse settlements. Consequently the former will soon outnumber them, and obtain a perfect ascendancy in the new state. As soon as they obtain it, they will be prompted by their habits, their feelings, their political principles, and their religious sentiments, to use it for prohibiting the further introduction of slaves, and providing for the gradual abolition of slavery. This course of things I take to be as certain as the connection of cause and effect. Further: Missouri is not a country adapted to the profitable employment of slaves, and few will go there. It is too far north for the advantageous cultivation of any of the great staples in which the labor of slaves is usefully employed. It commences at lat 36° and extends to 40°. Neither sugar nor rice will grow as far north as 36; a little cotton may be cultivated in the southern parts of the state, for domestic use; but this plant is so much better adapted to more southern climates, that all who wish to cultivate it for sale will go to the states south of Missouri, or to the territory of Arkansaw, where their slaves can be more profitably employed, and lands will be equally cheap. The same remarks will apply in a great degree to tobacco; for which the northern parts of the state, on the Missouri river, where the best lands are to be found, or there is at least far the greatest proportion of good land, are, I have no doubt, too cold. I mean too cold for its profitable cultivation, as an object of sale and exportation; for I know that tobacco will grow much further north. It may, perhaps, be cultivated to advantage in the southern parts of the state; but there, as I understand, the quantity of good land easily brought into a state of cultivation, is not considerable. A great part of the country is low and marshy, requiring great labor and expense to drain, reclaim and improve it. This labor cannot be profitably performed by slaves; it requires the hands of hardy and industrious freemen, who work for themselves, and are content with a slow progress and gradual success, because they look to the future enjoyment of the fruits of their toil and self–denial. These reasons will induce emigrants who are slave owners, to look south of Missouri for new settlements, and slave owners who are now there either to go with their slaves in the same direction, or sell them to persons who will purchase them with that view. A few may be retained as domestic servants, or to assist their masters in the improvement and cultivation of farms; but the number cannot be considerable. The effects of these causes will be very much increased by the great distance to market, and the heavy expense of transporting bulky articles of produce, even when aided by the current of the Mississippi and steam navigation—A transportation of near two thousand miles must under any circumstances be very expensive, and will furnish another powerful inducement, for the removal of the slaves further south.

These two circumstances, Mr. President, the approaching, if not the actual, preponderance of eastern and northern emigrants, and the insuitability of the country for the profitable employment of slaves, I feel confident, would restrain the increase of slavery, and soon put an end to its existence, in the state of Missouri, without the interference of Congress. But in addition to these considerations, which I deem of great weight, there is another far greater, to which I will now advert. The objection to the toleration of slavery in Missouri, which I am now endeavoring to answer, consists in its supposed tendency to augment the whole number of slaves in the United States, and thus to increase the evil of slavery under which we now labor, and which I admit to be already great and alarming. No person indeed can be more sensible that I am of its magnitude, or more desirous of mitigating, diminishing, and finally removing it, by all practicable and proper means. But I do not believe that it will be increased by its extension to Missouri. Indeed I think, and will presently attempt to show, that it will be mitigated and diminished on the whole. How is it to be increased I would ask? There is but one way, and that is by increasing the whole number of slaves in the U[nited] States. This it is contended would be the effect. It is contended that the slaves, if thus spread over a larger surface, will upon the whole multiply faster, than if they were confined to the country on this side of the Mississippi, and the state of Louisiana. This I consider as an error produced by the misapplication of a celebrated axiom to political economy, commonly called the principle of Malthus; not because Malthus first discovered or advanced it, but from his having been the first to define and explain it, and to make it the basis of a system. This axiom teaches that the inherent tendency to increase in the human species, is restrained by nothing but the want of food: that population is constantly pressing on the means of subsistence, its only effectual barrier: and consequently that if you diminish the number of people in any place, while the ordinary means of obtaining subsistence remain the same, the void will soon be supplied by the natural increase of the species. This is undoubtedly true. It is proved and exemplified by the case of every well governed country, which has maintained destructive wars, or planted and peopled extensive colonies; and by none more thoroughly or clearly than that of our eastern states, especially Massachusetts proper and Connecticut, which, without diminishing their own population or preventing its gradual increase, have furnished a perpetual and copious supply of emigrants for all the unsettled territories in their vicinity, as well as for those northwest of the Ohio. It is also inferred from this axiom, as a corollary equally certain with the first, that if you leave all these emigrants at home, the population of the parent country will increase no faster and no more, than if you take them away; because this population being regulated by the ordinary means of subsistence, or, more properly speaking, by the facility of obtaining subsistence, cannot rise above a certain point, and will attain that point. This is true in some cases, but not in all—and here, I apprehend, lies the fallacy which I am endeavoring to detect. It is true in relation to those countries alone, which, according to their institutions, state of manners, modes of life, and system of agriculture, produce as much subsistence for man as they are capable of producing: which, in other words, are full of inhabitants and can maintain no more, without improving their agriculture so as to make the same land produce more food; establishing manufactures for the purpose of exportation, with which food may be procured from abroad; or engaging in commerce, fisheries, mining, or other similar pursuits, which may produce the same effect. But it is not true in relation to countries which have an abundance of uncultivated land fit for cultivation, and interspersed through every part of them. In such countries new land may be reclaimed and the cultivation constantly extended, without any great improvements in the mode of cultivating, or any considerable change in the habits or system of life; and this extension may go on till the whole of the land fit for cultivation shall be brought into a productive state.—While it is going on new supplies of food will be furnished, as fast as mouths to consume it are brought into existence. It will always be abundant, and consequently the expansive powers of the human species will not be checked or restrained. I will ask if this is not the situation of all other slave holding states, even in their most populous sections? Whether they have not every where abundance of land fit for cultivation and still uncultivated, not to speak of those vast regions almost untouched, which are open in the southwestern states, and will furnish for ages to come, food and profitable employment for all the slaves which can be removed from the quarters where they most abound? There is no doubt of the fact. What then would be the effect of keeping the slaves out of Missouri, and the other territories west of the Mississippi? That they would multiply the faster on the east side, where they would clear more land and produce more food, enough for ages to come, to feed all the mouths that population, with all its inherent energies, can supply. What will be the effect of removing a part of them beyond the Mississippi? That they will increase and multiply there, instead of increasing and multiplying here; and that the whole amount of their increase will remain the same for many ages to come. In other words, that whether they are excluded from Missouri and Arkansaw, or not, their number in the whole United States two centuries hence will be the same. This seems to me to be long enough for us to look forward; on this subject, at least. If the people of those countries find slavery an evil, they will abolish it long ere then. If they should desire to have slaves, they will long ere then find the means of introducing them, whatever we may now think or do on the subject.

The next objection to be noticed, and which involves considerations of a very important and interesting nature, applies to the supposed tendency of the measure in question, the introduction of slaves into the state of Missouri, to increase what is very inaccurately termed "the slave representation" in the federal government. It is well known that under the federal constitution the number of representatives and of electors of the President, from each state, is in proportion to the whole number of free persons and three fifths of the slaves in each. This representation in proportion to three fifths of the slaves, is inaccurately and often invidiously termed "a slave representation," but it is not so. It is a territorial representation, in the adjustment of which the number of slaves was adopted as the most convenient regulation. The southern states, where this species of property unfortunately prevails, have local interests different in many important points from those of the states in the north and east. As they were far less populous, and must long if not always continue so, a mere numerical representation in the general government would not have afforded protection to their peculiar rights and interests. They therefore insisted on a representation in some degree territorial. The other states yielded to the justice of this claim, and as a fixt number of representatives and electors in a community constantly increasing, and increasing with different degrees of rapidity, in different places, would soon have become very unequal and unjust a measure or regulation was adopted, which was of a nature to increase with the general increase of the community. This regulator was the slaves, and it is not easy to perceive how a better one could have been found. It is however very far from being a favorable one to the slave holding states, as will presently appear. Such as it was, however, no better one could be found, and it was adopted, not as a representation of slaves, but as the measure and regulation of a territorial representation. This idea of a territorial representation, for the protection of local rights and interests, is familiar in our governments. It occurs in this state, where some of the counties are much larger and more populous than others, and yet all have an equal representation. The small counties are for the most part in one section of the state, and the large ones in another; and these different sections have different local interests. The territorial representation protects their interests. If it were purely numerical, the section of the small counties would be governed by the other. A mere numerical representation is hardly any where admitted, and if it were it would often operate most unjustly. If the city of Philadelphia, for instance, had a number of members in the Pennsylvania Legislature, in the full proportion to its number of inhabitants, it would almost govern the state. The same observation will apply to New York, Baltimore, or any other large and populous capital. Who will say that London, with its twelve hundred thousand people, ought to send members to parliament in the full proportion of its numbers? Nor is this idea of territorial representation, for the protection of local rights, confined in our constitution to the ease of the southern states, or to the House of Representatives. It is the votes of the state representation in the senate, which is strictly territorial. Each state, however small, had separate rights, and for their protection each was allowed an equal representation in the Senate. I have made these remarks to show, that the territorial representation in the southern states, regulated merely by the number of slaves as a convenient measure, and often held up in the most invidious and odious light, as placing slaves in one section of the Union on a footing with freemen in the other, is a just and necessary measure for protecting and securing the peculiar local interests of the southern states, and ought to be treated with more indulgence. How effectual it was in attaining its object, and how likely to prove detrimental to the other sections of the Union, I will presently take occasion to consider. My object now is to enquire how far it is likely to be exercised, absolutely or relatively, by the extension of slavery in Missouri, or beyond the Mississippi.

If I have succeeded in the attempt to prove that the increase of slaves in Missouri cannot increase their whole number in the Union at large, because if they were not carried over the Mississippi they would increase just as fast on this side; it follows as an undeniable and evident consequence, that their extension beyond the Mississippi cannot increase the whole amount of the territorial representation, improperly called the slave representation. A given number of slaves, one hundred thousand, for instance, will give the same number of representatives and electors, whether part of them are beyond the Mississippi, or they are all on this side. This representation would be divided among a greater number of states, which might, perhaps, be a benefit, but it will be precisely the same in its aggregate amount, in one case and in the other. This is too obvious to need illustration.

But admitting my opinion on this point to be unfounded; admitting that by the extension of slavery beyond the Mississippi the whole number of slaves, and consequently the whole amount of slave representation, will be augmented; there is another and far more important view of the subject, derived from more obvious if not more certain principles, which I will now proceed to present. The alarm about the slave representation proceeds from the supposed danger of its exercise, should slavery be permitted to spread into the new states beyond the Mississippi. It is however not from the position but the relative exercise of this sort of representation, that danger can be apprehended. If the free representation, or rather the representation in the states where there are no slaves; be found to increase still faster than that of the slave–holding states, it is quite clear that the advantages originally accorded to the latter, or more properly the security and protection originally provided for their local rights, are continually diminishing. If for instance at the outset of the constitution the slave holding states had fifty representatives, and the others the same number; and at the end of twenty years the former with all the increase of their slaves had sixty representatives, and the latter eighty; it is quite clear that the proportion or balance originally established among them is destroyed, and that the non–slave holding states to say the least, are in no danger of losing any portion of their original rights or influence, by the exercise of slave representation. Now what is the fact? I answer let the census speak.

It appears from the census of 1792, the first taken under the present government, that Delaware, Maryland, Virginia, North and South Carolina, Georgia and Kentucky, the seven slave–holding states then in existence, had among them forty–eight representatives; and that New Hampshire, Massachusetts, Rhode Island, Connecticut, Vermont, New York, New Jersey and Pennsylvania, the eight non slave holding states, had among them fifty seven—nine more than the others. By the last census, that of 1810, the same seven slave holding states have sixty two representatives, an increase of fourteen, while the same eight non–slave holding states have ninety seven, an increase of forty. One class of states has obtained an augmentation of about one third; the other of almost two thirds. The difference between them at the first period was nine; at the second thirty–five: and this not withstanding the existence of the slave trade in the two most southern states, during a great part of the period. This result may create some uneasiness in the southern states, who thus see the defences erected for their local interests and rights, in the territorial representation, crumble and waste away; but what just cause of alarm it can afford in the other sections of the Union, I am unable to perceive. And this change to the disadvantage of the slave holding states must go on, with an accelerated and accelerating velocity. It arises not from accident, but from causes inherent in the state of the country, and the nature of man. It is an undeniable and a melancholy truth that the existence of slavery retards population by retarding the improvement of the country. How it produces this effect need not now be explained, although the explanation would be very easily given, but the fact is undoubted. Freemen work more than slaves, because they work for themselves, and save more, because they save for themselves—As they cultivate better they require less land, and consequently form more compact settlements. As many more of them follow handicraft trades, they form a much greater number of towns and villages. Hence the same quantity of land, of equal quality, will support a much greater number of free people than of slaves.

So far the cause of the greater increase in the representation from the non slave holding states lies in the nature of man. But there is also a very powerful cause in the nature of the country. That part of it where slavery exists, the southern states, is in general far less capable than the other is of a dense population.—The soil in general is poor, but the country is intersected by veins or stripes of very rich land, which commonly lie along the streams and rivers. These stripes or veins are very inconsiderable in quantity, when compared with the middle grounds, though very superior in quality. They are almost wholly occupied by wealthy slave owners, and employed in the production of staples for exportation. The middle grounds, constituting more than four fifths of the whole surface in many places a much greater proportion, consists of land too poor for profitable cultivation, frequently unfit to be cultivated at all, and are of course very thinly peopled. This description appears to almost the whole alluvial country of the southern and middle states, from the Delaware river to the Sabine; including a very large part of the states of Delaware, Maryland, Virginia, the Carolinas, Georgia, Alabama, Mississippi and Louisiana. The lower, or alluvial country, of all those states; that is the country lying below the falls of the rivers, is almost wholly in this situation. There are some tracts and districts of a different character, but they are very inconsiderable when compared to the great mass of the slave country. In travelling through that country, in some of its oldest and most improved settlements, you have a fertile, well cultivated and populous tract, on the banks of a river, where wealth, elegance, and luxury abound, and after passing over a sandy plain, covered with pines, and almost destitute of inhabitants, you reach another populous and wealthy settlement, extended in two lines along another river. The middle ground is seldom less than ten, and often twenty miles wide; the fertile tracts seldom more than two or three; and in some places you may travel half a day without seeing a human habitation. Such countries must long remain very thinly peopled.—They are indeed in many parts in a state of decay; and if within the last twenty or thirty years the southern and some of the middle states have increased considerably in population, the increase has taken place in the western parts, where slaves are comparatively few, and the nature of the country is very different.

What, on the other hand, is the character of the northern and eastern states, in this respect? They are, almost everywhere, capable of compact settlement, and of supporting a dense population. Almost the whole surface of New York, vast as it is, admits of profitable cultivation. The same may be said of the states northwest of the Ohio; and it will apply though not in quite the same extent; to the unsettled parts of Maine, New Hampshire and Vermont. Pennsylvania is more encumbered with mountains, but there are still large tracts of unsettled and fertile land in her plains, and a very large portion of her mountains themselves is susceptible of cultivation.

Thus it appears, that the advantage gained by the non-slaveholding states over the others, in their number of representatives, notwithstanding the slave representation, is in its nature progressive. It is derived from the nature of man and the character of the country, and must go on. In eighteen years, from 1792 to 1810, the non-slaveholding states have increased in their number of representatives at the rate of 66 per cent, and the slaveholding at the rate of 33, notwithstanding the importation of slaves into some of them during a great part of that time. The former had gained forty representatives, and the latter fourteen. The census which produced this difference still operates, with increased and increasing force—while the suppression of the slave trade will check the increase in the southern states. In the approaching census, soon to be taken, it will be seen, that the slave representation, in more correct language, the territorial representation, of the southern states, allowed to them for the protection of their local rights and interests, has already diminished at least one half in its relative, that is, in its really effective amount, and must undergo a further and continual diminution. On which side then, in what quarter, is the cause of alarm, on the subject of this species of representation? It is already reduced to less than one half of its relative, that is, its effective amount, in the short period of thirty years; and causes of reduction as steady as the progress of nature, are still in operation. They must very long continue to operate; as long, indeed, as there shall be new lands to clear and cultivate in the northern, eastern and western sections of our country, and as the growth of manufactures in the old and populous settlements, shall enable them to go on increasing their numbers, by obtaining food from elsewhere, in exchange for the products of their industry.

Let them dismiss their unfounded alarms, about the exercise of what they call the slave representation, through the extension of slavery in Missouri. They may be assured that it will not extend farther, nor exist long; that if it should both exist and extend, it will not augment the whole number of slaves in the United States; because if they do not go to increase and multiply on the other side of the Mississippi, they will increase and multiply just as fast on this side; and that if their whole number should be augmented, so as to augment the whole amount of the slave representation, that augmentation can never keep pace, with the far more rapid and extensive increase of the non slave holding population; can never maintain its present ground, much less regain any part of that which it has already lost.

As little foundation, is there, in my opinion, Mr. President, for alarm about the increase of slaveholding states; which, it is apprehended by some, will augment to a dangerous extent, the influence of slave owners in the Senate of the United States. The number of slaveholding states has indeed increased, and may still increase. Their number in 1792, including Kentucky, was seven. Four have since been added; Tennessee, Louisiana, Mississippi and Alabama. Missouri and Arkansaw may and two more, and make the whole number thirteen. But this increase is fully countervailed by that on the other side. The original non slaveholding states were eight in number. To these three have already been added; Ohio, Indiana and Illinois: so that the two interests are now equally balanced in the Senate, each possessing 11 states. But this balance will soon be lost. There can be but two more slaveholding states, within our present territory; Missouri and Arkansaw. On the other side, there will be at least four; one of which, Maine, is ready to step into the Union—and another, Michigan, will soon follow. The country north of Missouri and west of the Mississippi, will, in process of time, form a third; and a fourth will arise, probably, at an earlier period, in the territory north of Illinois, east of the Mississippi and west of lake Michigan. The two sections are now equal. Missouri and Maine coming in about the same time, will keep them so. Arkansaw and Michigan will probably advance with nearly equal steps, and when they come in, the equality will still be preserved.—But there it will end. The two states north of Missouri and Illinois, where, by the way, there will probably be four hereafter, instead of two, will give the preponderance to the non-slaveholding section; and as there will be room for no more new states in the south, this preponderance will be perpetual. It will not be disturbed by the acquisition of Florida, should we hereafter make it, which seems probable; because that country will not be sufficient for more than one state, and it is certainly within the limits of possibility that its weight may be overbalanced by far more extensive and important acquisitions in the north.

Before I quit this part of the subject I will notice another cause of alarm, supposed to exist in the great extent of the country belonging to us west of the Mississippi. This boundless space, as it is sometimes called, is represented as a vast threatre, on which slavery, if not now excluded, would hereafter exert and extend its baneful influence. This is very eloquent, but not very exact. The country in question is indeed of vast extent, in a mere geographical view: but the part of [it] fit for cultivation and settlement is far from being considerable; and of that part the southern portion only, that portion which lies south of latitude 40° is suitable for the employment of slaves. The country thus fit for settlement extends along the Mississippi from its mouth to a high northern latitude, and is not more, as I understand, than two hundred and fifty miles wide, on an average: probably not more than two hundred. At that distance west of the Mississippi you reach the great natural meadows, which extend west many hundred miles to the foot of the Stone Mountains. This vast tract is every where entirely destitute of wood. It has very little water, except the rivers which rise in the Stone Mountains, and traverse it in their course to the Mississippi. These defects must forever render it unfit for the habitation of an agricultural people. A new race of Calmurks may wander over it with their herds, keeping near to the rivers, and shifting their temporary habitations as the want or the abundance of pasture may direct; a few hunters may roam through its vast solitudes, in pursuit of the wild animals which it supports; but agricultural settlements cannot extend beyond the line, which divides it from the wooded country. Here is found the limit of our empire. Thus far, we can go, and no farther. Those scattered and wandering tribes of herdsmen or hunters, may acknowledge some loose dependence on our government, and pay an occasional and imperfect obedience to our laws; but our effective progress westward must here stop. In the vallies of the Stone Mountains, and on the banks of the Columbia and its branches, a new nation may hereafter arise, of American or of Russian origin; but it will not be a part of our confederacy, nor subject to our dominion.

These alarms then, about the countless multitudes of slaves which are to arise in the boundless regions beyond the Mississippi, unless the entrance be now barred against them, may all be dismissed. There is room there but for three states of moderate size, within the limits where slaves can be profitably employed. One of these is Missouri, whose western boundary extends as far as the habitable country. It has already been seen that it cannot be expected long, to continue a slave holding state. Another is Louisiana, which extends west to the western boundary of the United States, and is essentially a slave–holding state. The third is Arkansaw, now in its infancy and very imperfectly known. It may be a slave–holding state, and is the only one really and permanently affected by this question. Louisiana is already one, and must continue so. Missouri will not long be one, in whatever manner the question may be decided.

Having taken this review of the chief objections to the further admission of slaves into Missouri, in the hope of being able to contribute something towards allaying or calming the apprehensions to which they have given rise I will now advert as briefly as possible to some of the considerations, which, in my judgment, rendered it inexpedient for Congress to interfere.

And first I would call the attention of the senate, to the doubts entertained in a large portion of the United States, and in Missouri itself, on this subject. Although I do not concur in these doubts, yet it is impossible to deny that they are entitled to very great respect. In a government like ours doubtful powers ought to be very cautiously and sparingly exerted; and never except in cases of very great importance: where the object to be attained is not only great but certain, as far as things of such a nature are capable of certainty. I have seen, in more instances than one, the injurious effects of exercising doubtful powers, in cases of mere speculative or conjectural advantage. Will any one after a full and dispassionate view of this subject, pronounce that the good expected from this interference of Congress or the evils to be averted by it, are, under all the circumstances of the case, either great or certain? I do mean absolutely certain, but certain, as the lawyers say, to a common intent.—Are there no evils to be apprehended from it? Consider the strong feelings excited by this question in Missouri. Consider the strong opinions there entertained, that Congress does not possess the constitutional power to exact this condition.—Is it of small importance to allay these feelings, and restore them by others of affection and confidence? Is there no risk in running counter to these opinions, sustained as they are by the opinions and feelings of nearly half the Union? Is it wise to commit the authority and try the strength of the general government in the attempt to enforce in this distant quarter, a provision believed there and by half the rest of the nation to be unconstitutional? A wise government would pause, one would think, before it commenced such a course, in the pursuit of an object which all must admit to be remote and in a great degree speculative. I will not dwell or enlarge on these topics. They suggest ideas of peculiar delicacy and interest, the mere mention of which I deem sufficient.

There is however one view of the case closely connected with this branch of the argument, which I do not feel at liberty to omit. The measure proposed and urged in Congress, if I recollect it aright, is not confined to prohibiting the future introduction of slaves into Missouri, from other parts of the United States, but goes further, and provides for the gradual liberation of those already there, or their descendants.—This is a most proper measure if adopted, as I have no doubt it soon will be, in both its branches, by the state itself: but to see it attempted by Congress will naturally excite, whether justly or not, and does excite, distrust and alarm in the slave holding states. They will naturally regard it as the commencement of a system, by which their rights of property are to be undermined, and what they consider as the main source of their prosperity must be dried up: as an entering wedge, by which the way may be opened to their rule. That they should be extremely sensitive on this point is natural, considering the opinions and feelings, religious and political, which they know to prevail in those sections of the union, whose relative and positive right in the national counsels increase with their population, so much more rapidly and steadily than their own. Is it wise, I would ask, to alarm this sensibility, which, whether well founded or not, is extremely keen, and to produce this dangerous alarm by measures calculated to guard against a very remote and problematical evil? Is not the alarm itself, and the party divisions by geographical lines which it is calculated to excite and to foster, a far greater and more certain evil, than any apprehended by the supporters of this measure? It is from this geographical division of parties that we have most to apprehend; and it seems to me, that we cannot too carefully abstain from every measure calculated to produce it.

The next consideration to which I will advert, as tending to render it inexpedient for congress to interfere in this case, is derived from their omission to interfere at the proper time. There was a time when they might have interfered, without exciting any doubts about their constitutional power—any dangerous feelings among the people of that country, or any alarms or apprehensions elsewhere. This country was ceded to the United States in 1803.—It passed under their actual dominion in 1804, by the transfer of the French government. It was then, as a territory of the United States, under the sole and absolute government of congress; which, in the exercise of its constitutional powers, divided the country into two territories, and established a territorial government in each. The lower territory, then called Orleans, now the state of Louisiana, extended up as far as the southern boundary of Arkansaw. The other, under the name of Louisiana, included the two territories of Arkansaw and Missouri, and all the country north and west of Missouri. This country was very thinly peopled, and contained very few slaves; not more, according to the best information I have been able to obtain, than one thousand or twelve hundred. It was then perfectly competent to congress, in the exercise of its plenary legislative authority, to interdict the further introduction of slaves. Such a measure would have excited no alarm, and no murmur. It would have been perfectly analogous to the course pursued in the territory northwest of Ohio, where slavery was interdicted immediately after the cession of that country to the United States. It could not have been completely interdicted in the territory of Louisiana, nor in Missouri and Arkansaw, because the people there were protected by the treaty of cession, in the enjoyment of their property: but the further introduction of slaves might have been prevented. The occasion, however, was suffered to pass by. Congress, by its silence on the subject, during fourteen years, sanctioned the introduction of slaves, and, in effect, held out an invitation to slave owners to remove thither with their slaves, and to purchase lands with a view to the introduction of others. By what fatality was it, that this evil was not checked in its infancy, while the power to check it was complete and undeniable; that it was rather encouraged in its growth then; and that the effort to check and eradicate it, was reserved for the moment when the power became questionable and could not be exercised, without exciting the strongest opposition in the country itself, and apprehension and alarm throughout the nation? This omission and delay were certainly unwise, if done with reflection, and most unfortunate, if the effect of inadvertency—Certainly they operated as an invitation to immigrants to go with their slaves into that country; and thus afford a strong additional objection to the measure now proposed.

It may be expected, Mr. President, that I should say something on the benefits to be anticipated, in the districts which abound with slaves, from the extension of them over a wider surface. After occupying so long the time of the Senate, I feel unwilling to press further on their attention, but this is a view of the subject which ought not to be wholly omitted. I will compress what I have to say on it, into a few brief remarks.

I have already endeavored to show sir, that to remove a part of the slaves beyond the Mississippi, does not tend to increase their aggregate numbers, in the United States, because there is room enough for them to increase and multiply on this side, for centuries to come, and the only question is, whether they shall multiply there, or multiply in the same degree here. But it will I think be admitted by all, who have the slightest knowledge of the subject, that in proportion as the slaves are dispersed, in proportion as they are less accumulated in masses and in particular districts, their moral condition and qualities are improved; and the political and moral evils to be apprehended from slavery are diminished. If, for instance, five individuals possess two hundred slaves each, on five adjoining plantations, these thousand slaves will certainly be very inferior, in a moral point of view, to the same number dispersed among five hundred farmers, each of whom has two; or some four or five and some none at all. They may not be more abundantly fed, more warmly clad, or better situated for the mere multiplication of the species; but they will enjoy more individual freedom, more actual liberty, more association with their masters and the families and equals of their masters, and more means of instruction, intellectual, moral, and religious: they will be governed with more ease, and consequently with less rigour, will occupy in short a higher rank in the scale of being, and become more respectable moral agents. This may not happen in every instance; because particular circumstances, on one side or the other, may check or vary the operation of general causes: but such will be the general tendency, and the general effect. The causes may be found in the nature of man in society, and are sufficiently obvious. In all similar situations they will operate in a similar manner, and in a degree proportioned to the degree of condensation on one hand, and of dispersion on the other. This principle applies to the political dangers resulting from slavery, as well as to its moral effects. It can I think hardly be doubted, that there would be more danger from a thousand slaves, collected together in a small district, than from the same number dispersed over two or three counties, among a much more numerous free white population. And if the fifteen hundred thousand slaves who now probably exist in the United States, were all concentrated in Maryland and Virginia, or in the Carolinas and Georgia, will any one doubt that they would be more formidable, than dispersed as they now are throughout all the middle, southern, western, and south western states?

Who can tell what servile wars, what severities, massacres, and exterminations, such a concentration would produce? The evil of slavery, in fine, exists among us. We have seen that its total aggregate amount is not increased by the dispersion of the slaves. Its intensity is certainly diminished; like an inflammation in the human body, which, if confined to one spot, or one limb, might be sufficient to produce gangrene, or the most painful and dangerous ulcers—while, if it were dispersed through the whole system, it would, perhaps, be too inconsiderable to be felt. The diffusion in this particular case may not, and, I believe, will not, produce much effect. It will, most probably, be too limited as to numbers, to do much good; for I believe, for reasons already before the Senate, that but very few slaves will be removed to Missouri: but its tendency, as far as it goes, I have no doubt, is beneficial, in mitigating an evil which we cannot cure. This view of the case furnishes, as I think, an additional argument, of no mean force, against the restriction proposed in congress.

Entertaining, as I do, Mr. President, these views of the subject, in explaining which so much at length, I fear that I have fatigued the Senate as well as myself, I shall concur most entirely and cordially in the resolution on the table, provided it be amended in the manner which I have proposed, so as to confine it to the single case of the condition respecting slavery now proposed to be exacted from Missouri. I will, therefore, conclude, by moving that the amendment be adopted.

N.B. The amendment prevailed, and the resolution was adopted.

D

Letter to the Reverend Leonard Bacon[*]

————•••••————

Baltimore November 8th 1824.

SIR

I had an interview with Doctor Ayres, soon after his return from the Eastern States and new York, in which he informed me of various conversations which he had there, on the subject of a plan for the education of young people of colour, as a preparation for their emigration to some other Country, where they may enjoy the real advantages of freedom and civilization. He mentioned you as one of the persons who had thought much on the subject; and were engaged or disposed to engage actively in prosecuting so benevolent and patriotic an enterprize. As both he and I have both long had it much at heart, and are now employed in devising means for its accomplishment, he was of opinion that some good might be derived, from a full communication of our views to you, which he strongly urged me to make; assuring me that it would be well received, and might lay the foundation for a concert of measures and union of means, from which the most beneficial results might be anticipated. In this hope I have taken the liberty to address you.

When the African colonization scheme was first set on foot, in this part of the United States, it immediately occurred to all those who engaged in it, that nothing more could be done by individual exertion, than to open and pave the way to show what might be done, and in what manner success was to be sought. The rest, they were sensible, must be done by the General or state governments, or by both united, under the influence and with the sanction of an enlightened public opinion.

To this object all their efforts have been directed. It embraces two operations. The first is to prove by actual experiment, that a colony of

---

[*] The manuscript of this letter, only the postscript of which is in Harper's handwriting, can be found in the Bacon Family Papers, Box 1, Folder 18, Manuscripts and Archives, Yale University.

civilized blacks may be established on the southwestern coast of Africa; that a suitable and healthy situation may be found, and procured by purchase from the natives, that the good will and good neighbourhood of the latter may be secured, and the colony thus placed in safety; that by proper precautions all danger to the colonists from the climate may be avoided; that colonists in abundance, and of proper character and description, may be found; that they may be transported to the colony at a moderate expense, which will be greatly diminished, when a regular and extensive commerce between this country and that shall be established; that the materials of such a commerce already exist to a very considerable extent, as well as a very favorable disposition for it in the minds of the natives; that both must increase with the increase of the colony, and the consequent discouragement and decrease of the slave trade in that quarter; and that the colony may very soon be placed in a condition to govern and protect itself, and not only to provide abundantly for its own wants by the products of its agricultural industry, but to have a large surplus for commerce with this country and Europe, which will furnish the means of a very gainful trade with the natives.

All this we consider as satisfactorily proved, by the experiment thus far made. The colony indeed is small, but it is healthy, composed of good materials, and firmly established; The attacks made on it by the natives, with greater force and in more extensive combinations than are ever again to be apprehended, were repelled when it was much weaker and less provided for defence than at present. The conduct of the natives has ever since been friendly and kind. They manifest a great readiness to trade, a great desire to be instructed and to procure instruction for their children, and the utmost willingness to exchange their labour for those articles of consumption and enjoyment, which they were heretofore accustomed to obtain by the sale of each other. The colonists, when the last accounts were transmitted, had not yet raised a crop, and consequently did not actually support themselves. But many of them had one in the ground, and almost all had received their allottment of land, which they were preparing for cultivation. Their subsistence, by their own means, may therefore be considered as secured.

On the essential article of Government the last accounts are highly satisfactory. The Government was in the hands of men of colour, elected by the colonists, and went on well. The number of applicants who wish to be sent to the colony, is much greater than can be received. They consist almost wholly of persons brought up and accustomed to live in the country, by agricultural employments, or those handcraft arts which are indispensable to an agricultural people. This is the class of emigrants which alone we encourage or receive. The population of the cities is not considered as suitable for such a settlement as ours. Hence the emigration to Hayti does not interfere with our plan; but rather works together with us, for the attainment of the same great end.

We therefore regard the first part of our object, which relates to the practicability of colonizing the blacks on the Southwest coast of Africa, as having been attained. The second is to show how it may be carried to such an extent, as to relieve the United States gradually and impercepti-bly, but effectually, from the great and growing evil of the black population, and thus to leave room and time for the white population to fill up the void, by its natural increase. We are very sensible that colonies of civilized Blacks, placed on the coast of Africa, in however limited an extent, cannot fail to be very useful. They place the colonists themselves in a far better situation, where they may be really and effectively free, and may enjoy all the advantages which naturally result, from freedom and civilization united. They rid this country, as far as they go, of an useless population, to say the least of it; which is generally vicious and corrupt, or exposed to the inevitable danger of being rendered so, by their own degradation and their contaminating communication with a degraded race. So far as these colonies succeed, they tend to lay a foundation for African civilization, and for the diffusion of knowledge and true Religion, in that benighted region. Consequently they are highly useful and deserving of encouragement, however limited their extent.

But the great utility of this enterprise, to this country, to the African race here, and to Africa itself, depends on its receiving such an extension, as gradually to embrace the whole black population of the United States. This we know requires indispensably the consent of those, who have an interest in the services and labour of this description of persons. This interest is a right of property as well secured by the laws, and as sacred in the eye of the Law, as any other right whatever. It cannot and must not be touched. But we believe that by a proper course of Measures, the consent of those who hold this property may be obtained; and to that object all our Measures are mainly directed.

To accomplish that object, and to effect the entire removal of the black and coloured population, we believe that we must turn our attention wholly to the rising generation. We must embrace them in a great scheme of Education, which may be gradually made to absorb them all, with the consent of their parents when free and of their owners when slaves, and may fit them all for transportation at a proper age. To set an example of this scheme of Education, to shew how it may be effectually conducted, is the next great object which we have in view. It is in this most important object that we wish and hope to obtain your assistance, and that of the enlightened and philantropic body with which you are connected.

For this purpose our plan is to establish what we call a seminary farm, which may serve as a pattern for similar institutions throughout the union, and especially in those states where slavery exists: which may show by experience and example what can be done, and how it ought to be done. We intend to purchase or rent a good farm, in a healthy and convenient situation with proper buildings for the accommodation of about one hundred children of colour, of both sexes. This farm we prefer having in Maryland, because the children as they grow up can be better governed, in a state where slavery exists. Dr Ayres whom you know, and who from his energy intelligence and experience is highly qualified for the task, is intended to have the superintendance of the Establishment. When it is ready, young persons of colour, between 10 and 14 years of age, will be received and educated.

It is believed and expected that as soon as the seminary can be opened, a considerable number of free colored children will be placed there by their parents; and that some, perhaps many, who are slaves will be sent by their owners. The conditions in which both descriptions will be received are, that they shall be so employed as to maintain themselves, while acquiring all the necessary improvement, till they arrive at a suitable age; and shall then be sent to the colony at Liberia, and settled there with the usual allottment of land.

The chief employment of the males, while at the seminary will be agriculture. They will cultivate the farm or assist in its cultivation, and its produce will be appropriated to the support of the Establishment. There will also be workshops established, for all the common handicraft trades, such as smiths shoemakers carpenters and others of the first necessity, where all such boys as are found to possess particular aptitude for any of these trades will be employed in them, under suitable instructors; and the proceeds of their labour will be appropriated in the like manner. The Girls will be kept in separate apartments, and employed under suitable female instructors, in all the departments of domestic industry, household occupations, household manufactures, and the various employments suitable for females of the laboring class. Such part of the product of their industry as may not be wanted for the use of the establishment, will be sold, and the proceeds employed in defraying its expenses.

There will be a school in which, at proper hours, all the young persons will be taught reading writing and the rudiments of arithmetic. Means will be devised for carrying further those boys, who display extraordinary capacity. All will be required to attend religious worship, and to receive religious instruction, at proper times: for which purpose a clergyman and a place of worship will be provided.

The most effectual means will be adopted and enforced, for preventing all improper communication between these young people themselves, or with others beyond the pale of the seminary. To render these means effectual, is one great object of locating the seminary in a state where slavery exists, and where alone the proper authority, for this and other indispensable purposes, could be exercised. The children, when slaves, will be given to the institution as slaves, to be liberated when at a proper age for colonization. When the children of free parents they will be bound, until they arrive at a proper age. On these conditions alone will either class be received.

As an encouragement to good conduct and industry, an account will be opened with each child, when placed in the seminary; in which it will be charged with its necessary expenses, including its board clothing and proportion of general Expenses, such as rent fuel taxes and superintendance, and credited with all its labour at fixt rates. The surplus will be invested in a Savings–Bank, to accumulate for the benefit of the child, and to form a fund for its outfit, on its removal at a proper age to the colony. This is regarded by us as a very important object. Its details will be troublesome and laborious, but it will be attended to with the utmost strictness.

Such is the outline of the Plan. The funds for purchasing a suitable farm, and commencing the operation, were at one time believed to have been provided. A farm every way suited to the object had been selected, and a treaty commenced for its purchase, with fair prospects of success. But a disappointment in relation to the funds has taken place, which compels us to suspend all further proceedings until new resources can be found. I apprehend no other difficulty. Young persons of colour, I am fully persuaded, may be very soon found in any desirable numbers, to fill up the seminary, and furnish a constant supply. Many slaveholders in this and other states, will, I am assured, make contributions in young slaves, as soon as the establishment is ready for their reception. A still greater number of free blacks will be eager to send their children. It is intended at first to receive those of unexceptionable character, without reference to age, in order to get the establishment into operation. When that object is accomplished, the regulation on the subject of age will be adhered to strictly.

No doubt is entertained, that in a short time this establishment may be made, not only to sustain itself, but to leave a surplus for its enlargement, and for other objects. It is hoped and believed that when brought into successful operation it will serve as a pattern for numerous similar institutions, throughout the slaveholding states, and in other suitable situations, to be established and sustained by the Government and supplied with pupils by the purchase of young slaves, with the public funds. Thus while the present and part of the next succeeding generations are left to disappear gradually, in the ordinary course of nature. Their progeny may imperceptibly be drawn from their degraded situations, fitted for an higher condition and transplanted without a shock or convulsion, or too sudden a change in the state of Society or of labour, to a soil and climate suited to their nature, where they may find a country, and in becoming citizens and freemen may confer incalculable benefits on the whole African race, and contribute as much by a mutually beneficial commerce to our wealth strength and prosperity, as they now do to that poverty and weakness which are conspicuous in the part of the United States which they inhabit.

> Such, Sir, is the outline of the undertaking in which I wish to interest you and your enlightened and philantropic friends in the East. Should you or they deem it worthy of further enquiry, I shall at all times be happy to answer any questions, and to give you such information or hints as may be in my power, In the mean time permit me to subscribe myself, with the highest respect,

The Rev.d L. Bacon.   Your most obedient servt.
                                                        Rob: G: Harper

Nov. 12th. Postscript. Since this letter was written intelligence has been received from Liberia, the colony in Africa, which is contained in the enclosed slip. Mr Gurley is the agent of the Colonization Society, and was sent by the Directors to Liberia, for the purpose of ascertaining the state and condition of the colony.

Rob: G: Harper

Enclosure:

FROM AFRICA.

The Rev. R. R. Gurley, Agent of the Colonization Society, has just arrived in this city, from the coast of Africa. He states that the Colony at Cape Mesurado is in encouraging circumstances. The natives have been peaceful, and there is no danger to be apprehended from them. The Colonists felt no more fear of being attacked by the Ashantees, of whose proceedings at Cape Coast we have heard so much, than we do.— They are so far removed, and there are such various obstacles between, there is no prospect of it whatever.

The Colony has suffered for want of medical aid, but the deaths have been comparatively few, ten or twelve since March last, and those of ordinary diseases. Those who went out from Petersburg, under Waring, have erected houses, and are now conveniently accommodated. Considerable land, also, has been cleared, and the Colonists, in general, have, on the whole, manifested great perseverance and industry. During the absence of Mr. Ashmun, who went to the Cape de Verl islands for his health, they moved on harmoniously under the directions of Lot Carey, Johnson, and Waring, three men of colour. Mr. Ashmun has since returned, and resumed his superintendance; his health being in a great measure restored. Mr. A. is spoken of as deserving great credit for his unwearied efforts for the good of the Colony.

Land has been apportioned to the settlers, and a satisfactory system of government established. The country is represented by Mr. G. as well as by all others, as being remarkable for fertility. Coffee, sugar, cotton, rice, indigo, may be cultivated to great advantage. Mr. G. brought with him a specimen of indigo, raised by one of the Colonists; also, of a peculiar kind of cotton, of a consistency like silk. Of this cotton, one of the Colonists from this city, whose name, on account of her character and industry, ought to be mentioned, [M. Poulson,] spun and knit him a pair of socks which will show of what the material is capable.

Mr. G. brought with him various proofs of the ingenuity of the natives; as pieces of cloth, baskets, &c. made of grass, manufactured gold, cotton, war utensils, &c. Several of these were from the interior, and were made by the Foulahs.

He visited Sierra Leone, and found the Colony in safety and prosperity. The Ashantee war is entirely beyond the Sierra Leone region; also, there is no connexion between that and the Cape Coast, except that both are governed by the British. On his way from Mesurado, Mr. G. spoke a vessel going to Cape Coast, with supplies.

Philad. Recorder.

Index